The Waldorf Main Lesson

Also by Eric G. Müller

Novels
Rites of Rock
Meet Me at the Met
The Black Madonna and the Young Sculptor: Mythic
Dimensions of Celtic Chartres

Children's Books
The Invisible Boat
The Invisible Boat and the Molten Dragon

Nonfiction
Drops on the Water: Stories of Growing Up from a Father
and Son (Coauthor: Matthew Zanoni Müller)
Do You Love Your Teachers? Memoir of a
Waldorf Teacher

Poetry
Coffee on the Piano for You
Frogs, Frags, & Kisses
Life Poems for my Students
Pilgrim Poet ~ Roaming Rebel

Play
Rounding the Cape of Good Hope

The Waldorf Main Lesson

Eric G. Müller

ALKION
PRESS

Printed with the support of the Alkion Press Fund

ISBN: 978-1-7340170-3-8

First Edition

Printed in the USA

Published in 2020
by Alkion Press
14 Old Wagon Road, Ghent, NY 12075
alkion-press.com

Title: The Waldorf Main Lesson
Author: Eric G. Müller
Cover design: Helena Zay.
Cover photo: Marla Tolz

To my students, their parents and guardians, colleagues, teachers, mentors:
One and all.

Contents

PART ONE

PART TWO

PART ONE

Introduction

"At the very least, adults in education need to take note and recognize the more lasting value of a broader, more holistic education rather than the mechanical, here-and-now obsession with academic performance; it simply does not work for children."[1]

~ Jonathan Jansen paying tribute to
great South African teachers

THE BULK OF THIS BOOK was written during the coronavirus lockdown, which forced the world to resort to virtual interactions via Zoom and other web conferencing tools. The irony was not lost on me that I was extolling the fundamental importance of teaching in a *real* and immediate environment, while our students were sitting at home navigating the new realm of online learning, staring into screens, seeing matchbox-frames of their classmates and teachers, only from the shoulders up, experiencing delays, bad connections, and no-shows; that I was praising the health-giving virtues of holistic education through the unique format of the Waldorf Main Lesson; that I was exploring what it means to be together with the children in an alive and living setting, where the teacher is able to gauge the students' subtly shifting reactions to the variegated aspects of the long morning lesson, where they can sense the refined mood changes and the general atmosphere in the room, a room consciously formed to create an aesthetically pleasing environment through lazured walls (transparent colors especially chosen for the age group), further adorned with meaningful prints by the masters and art work by the students, as well as blackboard drawings, diverse scented plant life, wooden furniture, and other appealing details; that I was alluding to imponderables, unspoken cues by the children, and nuanced responses by both the students and the teachers. And lastly – that I was writing about an educational method that aims to support the freedom of the individual within a community based on love, respect, and social interaction. Yes, that irony was not lost on me, though I felt a great sense of loss.

Writing during the throes of the pandemic has underscored the importance of everything that has to do with real-time *human* connections, of seeing and being seen, of learners and teachers gathered together in the name of the highest ideals, without any barriers, immersed in the communal warmth of intimacy, and of breathing shared air – carrier of light, music, speech – and soul dispositions. An education that strengthens the immune system in order to ward off susceptibility to outer viruses that will undoubtedly continue to threaten us. The Main Lesson that includes movement, music, poetry, imaginative learning, and espouses the benefits of a sound sleep life and a nutritious diet, encompasses the well-known stimulants that support a healthy immune system, both physically and mentally.[2] In an interview with *Campus A, Stuttgart*, Michaela Glöckler, talking about the effects of the coronavirus, says, "Since the 1970s, it has been well established that our immune system reacts positively to positive good feelings, such as: joy, devotion, humor, thankfulness, appreciation."3 And that is exactly what pulsates through the Main Lessons – an antidote to all the fear and hate that weakens the immune system.

Every day as I sat down to write I had to think of the millions of students around the globe, including Waldorf students, who have been asked to turn on their computers and receive online assignments and lessons in a home environment that is not necessarily conducive to learning, especially in low income neighborhoods. Given the odds, so many teachers have been incredibly inventive, creative, and caring, going above and beyond the call of duty, putting in endless prep hours and having to learn and adapt to a whole new system of teaching. But what must the effects be on the students when even the adults are suffering from what has been termed "Zoom fatigue" or "Zoom gloom."4 And what is even more disconcerting is when politicians and wealthy backers in their zeal to "reimagine education," focus on virtual learning as part of the "new normal," which would disconnect people even more from one another, to the potentially disastrous detriment of humanity. That would be like falling through a hole, instead of going through a portal to new possibilities of working for a cleaner environment, more humane working and living conditions, and radically improved treatment of animals. The increased digitalization would exacerbate the feeling of isolation that many young people already experience, leaving them empty and unsatisfied, thus always on the lookout for some sensation to fill the vacuum. Dr. Michaela Glöckler:

> [It] is very important that we make it clear to ourselves that digital technology is not healthy for the neurological development of children and adolescents. They need to spend their developmental years in the real world before they accustom themselves to the virtual one [...] because the ability to think independently requires 16 years of healthy

brain development. In fact, the frontal lobe needs 15 to 16 years to develop to the point where one possesses the capability of self-control and independent thinking. In order not to lose sight of this we will have to think carefully and pay much attention when the current lockdown comes to an end. We mustn't allow ourselves to suppose: "we no longer have a need for many of the things in the real world. Now one can induct children and youth straightway into the online world." That would be very bad. And last but not least, in the name of pandemic-management, the move toward the total surveillance is currently being rehearsed – this is simply a fact – up to the point of enforced lockdown and monitoring us via our cellphones."[5]

Given the surreal "Brave New World" backdrop, I felt my words infused and charged with greater intentionality. I became acutely aware that what the world needs, more than ever, is an education based on authenticity and deepened, human-based insights. The global lockdown is a symptom of what we are up against, what we will have to face in the future, and what will come toward us from the outside with increased vehemence – multifaceted threats on education and thus human development. All the more reason to intensify and broaden our understandings into some of the crucial aspects of Waldorf education, such as, in this case, the Main Lesson, which we cannot afford to take for granted. The Main Lesson is key to understanding and embodying the educational underpinnings that is meant to rejuvenate education far into the future. As alluded to, it is not a given that we can continue teaching in such a relatively free and unencumbered way in the future. Governmental restrictions, the media, increased socio-political pressures, distracting and increasingly sophisticated devices, and sundry other hindrances have been encroaching slowly but steadily onto the field of education, adding to the fragmentation that is already so rampant in schools worldwide.

I am aware that my explorations into the theme of the Main Lesson are incomplete and colored by my own experiences, observations, leanings, and studies. Though I endeavored to be as comprehensive as possible I know that the results do not cover everything. Much more work is needed to fill out the picture. Some anthroposophical and "Waldorf" terminology is used, though I expect that most people reading this book will be somewhat familiar with the language. May this undertaking encourage and stimulate readers to arrive at a fuller and deeper understanding of the Main Lesson's potential and its special place in Waldorf education.

---

[1] Jonathan Jansen with Nangamso Koza and Lihlumelo Toyana, *Great South African Teachers: A tribute to South Africa's great teachers from the people whose lives they have changed* (Johannesburg: Bookstorm and Pan Macmillan, 2011), p. 11

[2] Michaela Glöckler, "The Corona-Virus and our Human, Health-Giving Forces." Eine Aufnahme des Campus A, Stuttgart. https://mail.google.com/mail/u/0/?tab=wm&ogbl#search/Andr/FMfcg xwHMsSvNKjgDjtZkTmWtbplNKMT?projector=1

[3] Ibid.

[4] Julia Sklar, "'Zoom fatigue' is taxing the brain. Here's why that happens." *National Geographic.* Science: Coronavirus coverage. April 24, 2020. https://www.nationalgeographic.com/science/2020/04/coronavirus-zoom-fatigue-is-taxing-the-brain-here-is-why-that-happens/

[5] Michaela Glöckler, "The Corona-Virus and our Human, Health-Giving Forces."

The Main Lesson

"There are no prescribed rules for teaching in a Waldorf School, but only one unifying spirit that permeates the whole."[6] ~ Rudolf Steiner

THE "MAIN LESSON," also known as the "Morning Lesson" is unique to Waldorf Schools and forms the foundation to Waldorf education throughout the grades. The focused concentration on one subject matter over a number of weeks allows for greater continuity. Already a few months before the founding of the Waldorf School, Rudolf Steiner introduced the idea of the Main Lesson in a lecture held on June 1, 1919, where he blatantly calls the fragmented existing school schedule the "nemesis of all genuine education."[7] He goes on to say: "[If we] think of bringing health to the educational system we must take care that the child remains with a subject as long as necessary."[8] On

August 15, 1924 in Torquay, England, he expounded on the
Main Lesson just as emphatically: "We thereby save the
children from what can work such harm in their soul life,
namely that in one lesson they have to absorb what is then
blotted out in the lesson immediately following. The only
way to save them from this is to introduce period [block]
teaching."[9] It also safeguards the *mood* that each teacher can
create and instill, made possible by the extended time of the
Main Lesson, without it being overridden by the next
teacher.

The vital role of the class teacher in the elementary
school applies most particularly to the Main Lesson. The
first two hours of the school day are devoted to this lesson
where the main focus is on one subject over a period of three
or four weeks, generally speaking, but can be as short as one
week and, in rare cases, as long as six or even seven weeks.
Usually it averages out to about nine or ten Main Lesson
blocks a year. The length of the block is subject to variables
and is mostly left up to the class teacher to decide, based on
the subject matter, time of year, the nature of the class, and
the overall pedagogical balance of the year. Rudolf Steiner,
at the beginning of the Waldorf School movement, suggested
various lengths with a review period at the end of the year,
but within a few years it evened itself out to three or four
weeks, and the review period was largely dropped. In the
high school, however, the Main Lesson schedule for the year
has to be carefully planned out, leaving little wiggle room
because most of the blocks are taught by different teachers
who are specialists in their field.

Each block is like a celebratory feast. Over the years I
have found the four-week rhythm to be the ideal. It feels
complete and whole. Three weeks feel rushed and I have to
guard myself against filling the shorter time with a four-
week work load. Inevitably, I find myself wishing for another
week of Main Lesson, which is often echoed by the students.
It is analogous to the lunar or tidal rhythms, where there is
a clear beginning and end after every 29.5 days, which

distinctly affects life on earth, both biologically and psychologically. It is not for nothing that some religious feasts are four weeks long, such as Advent. Four weeks allows for the soul-spiritual experiences, which have been imparted during a Main Lesson, to be imprinted into the life organism.[10] The content has had enough time to settle. It is similar to a season. The first week serves as an introduction and can be likened to spring. During the summer and fall of the second and third week, the main body of the material is presented and developed. The fourth week is like a denouement, where all the diverse threads are drawn together, the themes explained, resolved, and harvested. I usually refrain from giving the students too much work during the fourth week, letting them bring the Main Lesson books to completion. The work is laid aside, like grains stored in a barn over winter, and the land is allowed to rest. Four weeks gives one ample time to cultivate and enter into the mood of a block.

Waldorf education is not a prescriptive education, but a living, organic, and human based education that addresses the whole child. It truly is a *soul, body,* and *mind* education, which requires that the teacher must be well prepared, awake to the moment, and acquire the ability to respond accordingly, all in the service of the human spirit. Not an easy task. However, the foundational Main Lesson allows for the optimal applications of these ideals. Its importance and overarching effectiveness are recognized by all Waldorf teachers, as are its main components, though its structure and implementations may vary.

It is called a "Main Lesson" because intense emphasis is devoted to one academic subject for a block of time, and not because it has greater value than any of the other lessons that generally continue on throughout the year, such as the languages, the arts and crafts, phys-ed, chorus, or eurythmy. The German term for the Main Lesson is *"Hauptunterricht,"* which alludes to the human head (Haupt), as opposed to "Kopf," which refers to the head (in a more general way) that we share with the animals. The "head" houses some of the prominent senses that connect us to the outer world and also to the brain, the instrument used for thinking. "Haupt" also means "main," and points to the main focus of a particular subject for a few weeks. Some teachers refer to the Main Lesson as the "head lesson."

Through the students' direct exposure to the respective subject matter in a living and imaginative manner, their will forces and feelings are stimulated, which then rise up and become conscious in their heads. Thus, the students receive something of academic relevance while developing soul capacities. The intellect is not focused on directly but addressed through the "art" of education, which speaks to the students' whole body experience.

This "Haupt" lesson thus received its name because it is primarily devoted to cognition – the *head* forces of understanding, knowledge and thinking – and that the main focus is devoted to one academic discipline over a period of a few weeks. "Epochenunterricht" is another term used in Germany for the Main Lesson, which roughly translates to "Block Lesson," because each subject is taught in blocks of time. We could also use the term "Block Lesson," or "Block Class," though it has an awkward ring to it. The so called "extra main" classes (also referred to as "practice hours") center more on repetition and the development of skills (though not exclusively). And, according to an ideal schedule, the afternoon classes are devoted to the arts and to movement. This is, of course, not always possible due to scheduling conflicts, which always arise. However, it is a schedule worth aspiring toward, and in some years, it works better than in others. As such, the day addresses the threefold nature of the human being: head, heart, and hands: thinking, feeling, and willing.

Generally (and traditionally) speaking, the Main Lesson as such is divided into three clear sections: 1. *rhythmical part* (attuning); 2. *main part*, which includes review, new material, and bookwork, and which is often considered as the essence of the main lesson (inbreathing); and 3. *story* (outbreathing). There are, however, variations to this threefold order, some of which diverge from this division. Adhering to the rhythmic structure of the Main Lesson appeals to the *will* nature of the human being, which, in turn, strengthens the *cognitive* senses (those that relate to clarity of speech and thinking), and is enveloped in pictorial content that speaks to the child's realm of *feeling*.

As we can see, the *main part* of the Main Lesson, though it represents and emphasizes the new material and the "head," is placed between the *rhythmical part* and the *story* section that relate more to the will and the feeling. However, they both serve and balance out the focus on the head forces: *heart* and *hand* in the service of the *head*. And the *main part*, which is more "head" oriented, nevertheless has "heart" and "hand" components. It's more a matter of emphasis than any definitive division. This framework provides a supportive structure for the teachers, and abiding by this daily rhythm strengthens the children.

The Main Lesson teachers are advised and encouraged to remain in contact with the special subject teachers, letting them know what they are working on. This can facilitate meaningful connections between the different subjects. The students experience the faculty working together as a whole and can see how all the subjects are linked together in myriad ways. It is a form of team teaching if the class teacher can incorporate and inform the other teachers of what is happening within the Main Lesson. It favorably supports harmonious integration between students and teachers, and ultimately unifies the school.

In the lower school, and to a much lesser extent in the high school, the structure of the Main Lesson always includes some sort of artistic activity, such as singing, recitation, recorder playing, movement, and drawing. However, the central focus is on the academics, albeit taught in an artistic manner. The arts help to support the intellectual content, help to make the student receptive, and keeps the imparting of knowledge alive. For example, while teaching the geography of the Far East, one can include a class on Asian painting. These activities will vary throughout the year, depending on the Main Lesson, the season, and the teacher.

The class teacher ideally teaches the Main Lessons for the first eight years (see "The Eight Year Journey" in Part Two), though it depends on the circumstances. Specialists in the humanities and the sciences, who teach in the high school, are sometimes asked to teach in the middle grades, contingent on the school and the availability of teachers. The Main Lesson has the potential of maximizing effective and efficient teaching. It allows for and requires *economic use of time*, and as such, encompasses the central question and theme of this brief book: *How efficiently is the Main Lesson utilized?* For Steiner the endeavor to *teach economically* was one of "utmost importance" and close to his heart, which he voiced repeatedly in lectures from 1919 onward.

> What we consider to be of utmost importance in the Waldorf School is that the teachers make use of their available lesson time in the most economical way, that they apply "soul economy" with regard to their pupils' potential. If one builds up the lessons along major lines of content, which pupils are able to follow without becoming tired, or at least without feeling overcome by tiredness, and if one can work against any oncoming tiredness by introducing variations of the main theme, one can achieve more than by following other methods for the sake of advantages these may possibly bring.[11]

Though there are many differences in the way a Main Lesson is presented in the lower, middle, and high school, the basic structure remains more or less the same. The Main Lesson has the potential of being a powerful pedagogical tool in the hands of the teacher, *if* the structure and intention is understood and handled artistically. An understanding of the structure is a prerequisite, just like a painter must have a thorough knowledge of the qualities of color, or the musician of music theory and command of the instrument. Once we know and understand the structure, we can also deviate from it, according to the freedom of the teacher, and the needs of the respective subject.

Generally speaking, the Main Lesson is divided into three parts, as mentioned earlier, though I am slightly altering the emphasis: The first part includes the Morning Verse and the "rhythmical part." Part two is devoted to recall and the presentation of the new material (which may contain the story material). Part three includes individual work and the practice of skills, often referred to as "bookwork." These three parts refer primarily to the elementary grades.

I have seen the greatest variety of Main Lessons, some of which don't adhere to the aforementioned or traditional structure at all, yet still work, since they are consciously *composed*, and because the essential questions have been asked: What is the essence of the block? What are the learning goals? How will it benefit them for life? What soul capacities will they develop? How will it strengthen them? What leitmotiv or central image runs like a red thread throughout the block? What makes this lesson so effective and why is it so important? How can we get the most out of these foundational lessons? For instance, some well-known and successful teachers I have known, often preferred to bring the "rhythmical part" after the presentation of the new material and immediately before bookwork.

The following questions also have to be asked: Where, how, and why do Waldorf teachers often fall short? What are the common mistakes teachers make? How can teachers reap the full benefits of a Main Lesson? Are Waldorf Schools in danger of weakening or even losing the Main Lessons? Are we teachers undermining this most effective pedagogical gift by not penetrating its full potential? These and other questions need to be raised periodically in faculty meetings, discussed between teachers, and covered in teacher education centers.

How we *use* the Main Lesson will depend on how we *view* the Main Lesson, and to what extent we understand its purpose. Now that we have passed the 100-year mark of Waldorf education and are becoming ever more global, we need to keep on reading the signs of the times – possibly more vigilantly than ever before – and in order to continue, we must remain innovative, relevant, and cutting edge. The centennial proved to be an apt time to return to the source of Waldorf education – to its roots – in order to examine the original intentions as an impetus to go forth into the future, consciously and newly enthused.

It is especially inspiring for Waldorf teachers to ponder periodically the image and meaning of the Grail sword that Parzival was given by Anfortas: how it could always withstand the first blow, but shattered with the second blow; how it could be renewed if the broken pieces were brought to the spring near Karnant, the *source*, and wetted in the stream, called "Lac" before dawn, after which the sword would be *stronger than ever before*. That imagination, if acted upon, will ensure renewal for all teachers, of which we are so in need. We remain, as a movement, always in need of a renewal— a reforged and stronger sword. And the Waldorf teacher's "sword" is *speech*. To steel our speech is a noble duty, especially as Waldorf teachers, whose tool is the tongue from which the words may acquire wings. Sometimes, it almost feels as if we have been cursed for not asking the "Parzivalian" question, and for not going back to the *source*. As teachers we must return to the indications given by Rudolf Steiner over and over again, to see *how* we can use them in new and inventive ways, if we want to achieve the effects envisioned by Steiner when he inaugurated Waldorf education for the coming ages. In the words of Christoff Wiechert: "I have formed the conviction through the years that the source, or spring, of renewal lies in the original indications and intentions of Rudolf Steiner. If this spring begins to bubble up in us, we will become viable for the future."[12] That source is the "lac."

The Main Lesson lends itself to the cultivation of healthy habits. As teachers we immediately sense the mood of the class, the life forces of the individual students and the class as a whole. Intentionally cultivated habits such as punctuality, the order of the day's activities, the verses spoken throughout the day, and other rhythms that run through the lessons, all contribute to the strengthening of the child's life forces, also called the *etheric* forces. The new material, the more "factual" content of the Main Lesson, which includes many of the more intellectual goals, represents the body of the class, which often remains undernourished, and is in need of renewed focus. Through the artistic presentations of the class, which includes animated discussions, songs, poetry, and music, we feed their feeling realm, and help to harmonize this more sentient realm, which we often refer to as the *astral*. And all the while, we are also addressing their emerging individuality, which is subject to the laws of human development. We have to know exactly why we are bringing a certain content to the students, how it will serve them, what soul gesture it has, and how it affects their growth, their incarnating individuality or *ego*.

The broad spectrum I am laying out in this writing is based on the suggestions by Rudolf Seiner and pioneering Waldorf teachers who helped to develop the curriculum. It also includes insights gained through innumerable discussions with other Waldorf teachers and mentors, studies over the decades in an assortment of workshops and conferences and, of course, my own experiences of over thirty years in the classroom. The students themselves, have taught me more than I will ever know.

There are different ways of going about the Main Lesson, its structure and build up. What is important, however, is that the teachers work out of the deeper insights that anthroposophy can give (the wisdom of the human being), their own strengths and aptitudes, the children in their care, and the changing times and conventions – all of which (I stress) needs to be *reviewed* periodically.

In order to strengthen and support the cognitive senses, thus making the students more *perceptive* (which will serve them later on in life when they are called upon to make weighty decisions and evaluate all sorts of situations in their professional and personal lives), it is prudent *not* to emphasize the intellect unduly in the lower grades, which only exhausts the children due to the inherent abstractions. Whatever is pushed prematurely weakens the students. It is exactly *because* we want the children to have a strong intellect and be endowed with the fully developed capacities for critical and analytical thinking that we avoid premature and top-heavy intellectualism. There is time enough for those faculties to come to the fore once the "ground" work has been achieved. Referring once more to *Parzival*: The young hero was allowed to "play" freely in the secluded forest, the wilderness of Soltane, where he could roam wheresoever he chose, and learn the lessons nature gave, which awarded him with uncanny strength and unlimited potential and promise. Once the *time was right*, he set out to fulfill his destiny, learning all the necessary worldly knowledge within 14 days, when he was introduced to courtly customs, the rules of knightly conduct, and chivalric codes by the grey-haired knight, Gurnemanz. What a wonderful image of education. What other knights learned over the course of fourteen years (from 7 to 14 as a page and from 14 to 21 as a squire), he learned in a fortnight: each year compressed into one day. This imagination highlights the importance of *age appropriate teaching*.

Indeed, we teachers do less teaching than we think. For the most part the students teach themselves, with our loving assistance. Our task is to provide the optimal learning environment. We create the right mood for the students to thrive in. Little children are not "taught" their mother tongue in the first three years of their lives; rather, they learn through imitation. Likewise, the students later on learn through the forces within them that rise up, prodding them to learn. It's a force as strong as the force that gets them to stand up – to find their uprightness. I often tell my high school students, "In one sense, I am not really teaching you anything, I am a facilitator of learning. You teach yourselves." I see myself as an opener of doors, allowing and inviting the students to step out into the garden of learning. I show the way, remove impediments, protect, observe what interests them, point out the wonders of the garden, lead by example and through love. We are on the journey together.

However, much of what we have to do is already a compromise of sorts, but let us not compromise the education of our children in areas where there is no need. We know what the goal is: outer, earthly knowledge and skills (as represented by the Arthurian stream), and the more imponderable peripheral knowledge that reveals divine spiritual truths (the Grail stream), giving rise to self-knowledge, which is ultimately a more inner realm. The children need both, and as teachers we need to give them both. These ends do not necessarily have a clear roadmap (especially in our fast-paced, ever-changing modern environment), but we can sense and see the distant castles, so let's run through the woods, cross streams and rivers, saunter over hills and over mountains, go off the beaten track – have trust in the fresh paths we forge with the children. Helping and guiding hands will direct us, step for step through the sacred wilderness, the "wonderness." Not only the children, but we, as teachers, grow "slowly wise." Like Parzival, we will make mistakes as teachers, and like Parzival, we have the power within us to persevere. And similar to the old hermit Trevrizent, we can tell them the stories they *need* to hear, stories of themselves, which is the human story that contains all the stories.

Whatever a teacher brings can become hollow over time, even some of the most hallowed hallmarks of Waldorf education, such as the Morning Verse or the review: reduced to form without content. Then it is not a matter of leaving it out, discarding it like a "sacred nothing," but of re-enlivening it. And the guidelines, recommendations, structures and forms of the Main Lesson that are outlined in this book only work in so far as we breathe life into them. In every aspect the class teacher, or the Main Lesson teacher in the high school, is free to form the pivotal Main Lesson in their own way. In the end it is all about pedagogical relevance, personal responsibility, and *how* we work with the foundational morning Main Lesson. It is the "red wheelbarrow" of Waldorf education – so much depends upon it!

Though the Main Lesson is generally divided into three sections, I have subdivided it into twelve smaller units, from the time before school all the way through to snack and recess. Much of what is delineated below is in regard to the first eight grades, though I reference the high school throughout. Within each Main Lesson the rhythm of the entire day is reflected, because it encompasses the three essential aspects of the human being: *head, heart,* and *hand.*

~

This morning (as of this writing), I said goodbye to an 8th grade student who was moving away and enrolling in another school. We were all sorry to see her go and we wished her the very best. I asked what she would miss most about Waldorf. She didn't have to think long before answering, "The Main Lesson." She paused, took a breath. "Definitely, the Main Lesson. I like the way we can focus on a topic for two hours every morning over a period of three or four weeks. It really allows us to get into a topic." And she added, "That only happens in a Waldorf School. Other schools just don't do that. Yes, I'm really going to miss that."

[6] Rudolf Steiner, *Kingdom of Childhood,* (Anthroposophic Press, 1995) Lecture Two.

[7] Rudolf Steiner, "Social Basis for Public Education," June 1, 1919, in *Education as a Force for Social Change* (Hudson NY, Anthroposophic Press, 1997).

[8] Ibid.

[9] Rudolf Steiner, *Kingdom of Childhood* (Anthroposophic Press, 1995), Lecture Four, p. 71.

[10] Wilhelm Hoerner, *Kosmische Rhythmen im Menschenleben* (Stuttgart: Urachhaus, 1990).

[11] Rudolf Steiner, *Soul Economy and Waldorf Education* (Anthroposophic Press, 1986), p. 300.

[12] Christof Wiechert, "Rethinking the Threefold Division of the Main Lesson." Translated by John Weedon. First published in the *Rundbrief* (Journal) of the Pedagogical Section, 2010. (Waldorf News: http://www.waldorftoday.com/2011/01/rethinking-the-threefold-division-of-the-main-lesson-christof-weichert/).

Before Class

"Be willing to be a beginner every single morning."
~ Meister Eckhart

A GOOD MEAL, we all know, begins long before we sit down to eat. This holds true to most worthwhile endeavors in life. Before we even touch the ingredients, we think about the quality of food and what kind of meal we want to serve: our vision fuels the intention. Once we have formed a picture, we can get started. We make lists, plan, and go shopping. Back in the kitchen, with the ingredients laid out, we can proceed according to the recipe, which will most likely be slightly altered according to our own taste, experience, and circumstance. As soon as we grate a lemon peel, cut into an onion, or chop the parsley, smells arise, which only intensify when we start to cook, bake, or fry. Anticipation is built up and it whets the appetite, which gets the juices going, especially for those for whom the meal is being prepared. Moreover, care is taken to set the table, to make it look beautiful and inviting. Before the first bite has been taken, the senses have already participated in this meal, stirring the salivary glands. Digestion begins through anticipation. A great deal has to be put in place for the meals we enjoy, with many people to thank, apart from the person preparing the meal. Even the humblest meal deserves thanksgiving.

Each Main Lesson is ideally preceded with the same kind of meticulous preparation, taking much longer to prepare than to teach. Steiner suggested that for each hour of teaching we should prepare for three. Of course, some of this preparation might take place while we go for a walk, sip tea, or have a conversation with someone that sparks new ideas that we can incorporate into our lesson. Extending that thought, one can posit without exaggeration that, in a sense, we are always preparing (see "Preparing for the Main Lesson"), even for lessons that we don't yet know we'll be teaching. What are the essential prerequisites?

Each and Main Lesson block calls for different modes of preparation. However, there are commonalities. First, we must form an overview of the subject matter and determine the main themes and goals. Depending on our own knowledge and circumstances, we might choose to prepare for some upcoming Main Lesson blocks during the summer. Over the summer vacations I would gauge what subjects needed the most work and do the necessary preliminary studies. For example, I did not know too much about astronomy, so I studied the evening and night sky all summer long before 7th grade (often taught in 6th grade). Another year it was chemistry, and so on. The preparation included discussions with other teachers who had covered the material already. Many teachers have invaluable information to impart. It certainly made my life easier. Apart from the knowledge, one receives teaching tips, shortcuts, notes, piles of books, and advice, which all together builds confidence. When the block finally arrives, we can begin looking at the day-to-day details.

Now that the knowledge has been acquired, ready to be conveyed to the students, a different element sets in. This is the more meditative aspect. For me that is still the most acute the night before the start of a new Main Lesson block. My school bag is packed. I have everything I need. I know what I will be presenting. I am excited and enthusiastic. I have made sure to clean and prepare the classroom space the afternoon before, maybe even added a blackboard drawing. Nevertheless, as teachers, we always have this nagging and lingering feeling that more is needed, that more could have been done: Will I find the right words? Will I be able to connect to the students? Will they be as excited about the content as I am? Will I remember everything? Will I have to refer to my notes (furtively, so they don't notice)? How smoothly will the lesson go? Even after three decades of teaching I still find myself asking these fundamental basic questions, and I'm still beset by doubt, which feels like a self-flagellation. One is never the ultimate master teacher. There will always be bum lessons. At least, that's true for me. What to do?

As a friend of mine likes to say: *let go and let God.* There's truth to that, irrespective of the quasi-religious connotation. It's hard to let go, because no matter how much one prepares, one could always do more, know more. However, letting go, even somewhat, is essential. Letting go is a form of relaxing. I do see something spiritual in every student, and the classroom is a sacred place for me. When I was a class teacher, the desk did become my altar (a passing remark by Rudolf Steiner that I took to heart). True, my desk tended to be a bit messy, but it displayed and bore the tools of my trade: pens, papers, colored pencils, sharpener, books, chalk, paper weight, paper clips, bowl of tacks, and so forth – accoutrements for my sacrament of sorts. Letting go creates a space for other elements to sink in, and it opens us up to more expansive ideas, the unexpected. Teachers too need to digest the lessons.

Over the years, I have tried to make it a nightly habit to form a mental picture of the classroom, a habit that I have continued to pursue as a high school teacher. I imagine the room filling up with students; I can almost hear them, and sometimes I converse with them in my mind. I take each one in – even if it's only for a nanosecond. This is followed by an invocation, a quasi-prayer, which can be summed up in four quotidian words: *may it go well.* But sometimes, in certain cases, I expand on that. It's like casting a positive spell on my upcoming lesson, a blessing: May I find the right words. May something surprising slip in. May I feel inspired! May I be receptive to what the moment needs. May I be imaginative, intuitive. May I receive help from the good spirit of the class? And then, I let it go again, followed by a review of the day (or vice versa), irrespective of whether I have been teaching or not. It is an opportunity to observe my actions during the day, and as a teacher it gives me greater perspective to how my teaching went. The questioning continues: Who needs more contact and attention? Did I miss a pedagogical opportunity? Where could I have been more encouraging? Why didn't I make more use of humor? Were the children joyful enough? Indeed, it is also a good opportunity to mull over problems, to take them into sleep life, and to trust that solutions and resolutions will be found upon waking.

The next morning, I quickly scan through my intentions and again visualize what's coming toward me, or what I am going toward. Interestingly enough, if I remain open and receptive, I often receive some gift or other from the realm of sleep: a novel idea that could support or enhance my lesson, a change in the order of my teaching structure, an assignment or activity that suddenly seems appropriate to the Main Lesson content. It could come while brushing my teeth, sipping tea over breakfast, stoking the fire, or putting on my coat. It is one reason why I avoid listening to the radio or any electronic media in the morning or do any kind of business, especially having to do with any devices (though I have missed some pertinent emails and messages because of it). Just the morning necessities. It lets the night linger on, it lets us be slightly more receptive to the wisdom of the night – what it can and wants to reveal within those ever so faint "trails of glory." It's too easy to smother these subtle

conveyors of the spirit with the all too worldly and
unnecessary distractions.

Within the diminutive minutes before I step out of the
house, I feel myself changing – altering into the teacher.
Outwardly, it's barely noticeable, but it constitutes a
concrete and palpable inner shift. It's not always easy, and
slightly painful on a sentient level. I've likened it to the
transformation of Clark Kent to Superman, or the Bruce
Banner alter ego transmuting into the Hulk. But mostly it's
just Eric changing into Mr. Müller.

Entering the Classroom

"The intellect divides us into our separate selves but the
heart, if rightly educated, reunites us again."
~ Francis Edmunds[13]

AS I DROVE BACK from Brittany one summer toward
Paris, I saw a promontory in the distance on which stood a
huge cathedral with two spires. I immediately knew it was
Chartres. I spontaneously left the highway and drove up to
the Cathedral of Chartres, parked the car and hastened
toward this architectural, late medieval wonder that I had
heard so much about and that had availed itself to me so
unexpectedly. I ran toward it but was brought to an abrupt
halt in front of the main portal. It was almost as if the two
formidable steeples had lifted their mighty arms and
cautioned me to stop. This cathedral was not something to
be rushed toward or through. Its power was palpable,
demanding proper respect. Reverence. Gently, but solemnly

admonished, I took a few slow tentative steps forward, gazing up and around at the myriad sculptures in the arched portals and beyond. Gradually, my road-harried mood altered. These figures dating back to the 12th century exuded a calm and inscrutable power. I was still in my early twenties, had not yet studied the historical background of Chartres or its spiritual significance, but I'd heard my parents speak of its cultural and spiritual standing, and I was aware that it was home to an ineffable Black Madonna. But I did not need to know much to experience the sovereignty of the architecture and the artistry that went into every detail of the stonework. The act of entering this sacred space called for an inner change and purification. My ancient self wanted to genuflect in front of this magnificent temple, but the modern me stepped forward, pushed open the heavy wooden door and entered the hallowed space.

Likewise, when I step into the classroom in the morning, I feel like I am entering a revered realm. I leave *civvy street* behind, consciously hang up the baggage of my personal self on a metaphorical hook, as Steiner advocated, and enter: the classroom, my little cathedral.

~

I elude distractions of any kind in the morning. When I drive to school, I also refrain from turning on the radio, and if it happens to be on, I switch it off immediately. It's as if the electro-magnetic transmissions destroy the space. Morning time is sacred. Although my drive at present is not long, it still allows for reverie, possible insights. They can come in a flash. Once I leave the house I open up to the day, slowly, like the petals within a calyx. I open to the people as I walk from the parking lot to the school – to other teachers, parents, and students. It's not always easy to wake to the day. My natural inclination is to remain huddled within my own thoughts, but a warm "Good morning," a smile, a nod, or moments of mutual recognition help the opening process. For years now, one of our teachers, now retired, has and still plays the accordion on the pathway to the main entrance of the school (except during inclement weather). The happy tunes are like a sonic salutation – a humble gesture with subtle reverberations, easing the waking process for everybody. I take note of the weather. We all know the difference in mood between a sunny, rainy, cold, or misty morning. One can almost anticipate the cumulative atmosphere of the students before entering the classroom.

In the Eugene Waldorf school where I guided my class through the 8-year cycle, a group of teachers would meet to say a verse together, as is the practice in most Waldorf Schools around the world. We would gather before the majority of students arrived, so as not to leave them up to their own devices. Steiner was critical of teachers gathering together for the verse while so many of the students were running around and left unsupervised. He strongly suggested that the teachers should arrive at school much earlier.[14] The morning ritual between the teachers is similar the world round. After greeting each other, one of us would read the appropriate verse from Rudolf Steiner's *Calendar of the Soul* – usually repeating it in the German original – the weekly verses that connect the inner life of the soul to the seasons of the year. Then we all recited the following Steiner verse:

> *We have the will to work*
> *That into this our work may flow,*
> *That which, from out of the Spiritual Worlds,*
> *Working in Soul and Spirit,*
> *In Life and Body,*
> *Strives to become human within us.*

The ethos of this moment of centering is health giving and strengthening. We recognize our common goals: the education of students placed into our care. This foundational daily meeting reinforces the shared and unifying spirit out of which we work. It does not need all the teachers to be present, but it supports all the teachers.

The Steiner verse that I personally find helpful to meditate on is:

> *Imbue thyself with the power of imagination*
> *Have courage for the truth,*
> *Sharpen thy feeling for responsibility of soul*

Sometimes, we also sang a song. I treasured these morning moments with my colleagues. It is a confirmation of our like-mindedness and it enhances the soul mood necessary to enter the classroom and meet the students. Such a gathering fosters the social bond between the teachers. Many conflicts could be avoided if teachers could sustain this kind of morning meeting, which serves as a moral foundation to the day. The body of teachers is strengthened and it helps in the mutual support of one another.

I like to be the first in the classroom, though it is not always possible. With a quick look around I assess the state of the room. There is usually something that needs tending, especially in the high school where many other teachers use my "home room." Often, I need to rearrange desks, sweep, open up the piano, clean the blackboard (I've become a stickler for clean blackboards), and so forth. As a class teacher I had more control over the classroom, though, inevitably, there was still something to be done, like removing some wilted flowers from the Nature Table, sharpening pencils, or quickly adding something to the blackboard drawing.

Soon enough the students begin to enter. Every day is slightly different, but it does make a difference if the room has been "warmed up," which imparts a feeling of welcome. Inevitably, the teacher needs to step out for a moment for any number of reasons, but by noticing the bag by the desk or that the lights have been switched on the students know that you are nearby and will feel held. They notice the slightest changes. "Ah, you put new flowers in the vase. Good, it was about time." Or, "You pinned our paintings up."

"You cleaned the sink." In fact, they are almost disappointed if they can't spot some slight alteration. Of course, some of the changes happened the day before, usually long after they'd gone home. This quality of them anticipating something new can start from the moment they enter the classroom. This could be achieved by writing a riddle on the board for them to solve, or a math problem. Of course, it depends on what grade you're teaching. In the high school I sometimes write a quote on the board, or something enigmatic, making them wonder what it has to do with the lesson. Everybody likes surprises. It stirs their curiosity.

Many teachers organize little activities before the beginning of class. Recently I sat into a first grade where some of the students enjoyed doing form drawings. In another class, on a sunny spring morning, the children jumped rope outside the classroom. String games are a favorite and much-loved morning activity in first and second grade, such as "Kitty Whiskers," "Jacob's Ladder," "Witch's Broom, and "Cat's Cradle." Another favorite is clapping games (usually introduced during "circle time" or in a games class), which children love to do, even in the higher grades. All these games can be played in pairs or in groups, and require a great deal of coordination. They take on a life of their own and always engender a great deal of mirth. And then there are the students who just like to sit quietly, drawing or reading a book. Every class usually has a well-stocked library.

The way teachers enter the classroom has its effects on the students. We help to create the mood that they feel embraced by. And I in turn, can immediately assess the wellbeing of the students.

Depending on the school's tradition the teacher will shake the students' hands singly on entering the classroom, or in unison once the bell has rung. As a class teacher I liked to have the class line up outside the classroom at starting time, so that I could officially greet them, one by one. It signaled the start of the day and added a note of formality.

Though it belonged to our daily routine it never became perfunctory, not once over the entire eight years. This morning greeting, though short, was a true meeting. In this respect, the words of the poet Paul Matthews echo the sentiment perfectly: "The meeting of ego to ego confirmed in a handshake – that feels real to me, as does the relationship of word to movement."[15] In this case, the teacher perceives and senses the children's developing egos, their burgeoning individualities, and they, in turn, meet and recognize the *authority* of the teacher, which stands as a representative of the teacher's strength of ego. As Willi Aeppli puts it: "The child really perceives the power of true authority in an adult. Yet, this itself, is nothing other than an enveloping image of the true ego. [...] May the teacher be for the schoolchild this natural, beloved, inwardly founded authority, on which the child can develop his future ego-sense."

Throughout the years it remained important to me to shake each student's hand, look into their eyes, and maybe say a quick word or two. This moment can serve as an ideal opportunity to cultivate the ego-sense. In those few seconds one can notice a great deal: Is their hair combed? Have they wash their faces? Do they appear sleepy or vibrant? Are their hands dry, damp, sweaty, soft, or rough? Is their grip firm or limp? Everything tells a story. How do they say good morning? In a strong or weak voice? Smiling or sullen? Is the eye contact brief, radiant, withdrawn, reticent, or nonexistent? If I perceived a need of some sort, a sadness or anger, I would try to weave something into my lesson that might address or alleviate the hidden burden (or speak to them in private later on). Or if a number of students were still not taking enough care of their hygiene, I would discreetly include an anecdote about the importance of cleanliness.

It was all the more disconcerting to hear Anthony Fauci (the Director of the National Institute of Allergy and Infectious Diseases – NAID) recently declare on the news (as of this writing): "I don't think we should ever shake hands again," just days after I had written the above section on the importance of shaking hands, but I couldn't help but make a note of his words. It promotes a limited view of human relationships, where each person is reduced to an object, a potential foe, carrying and spreading germs, viruses.

Back in the days of ancient Egypt, Greece and Rome, shaking hands was considered a sign of peace, friendship, and trust. Are we forever going to forego mutual trust? Over the next few days I heard him repeat that same sentiment in different forms. Of course, it was said in connection to the coronavirus disease, but it shows unawareness of the profound power of touch for the wellbeing of humanity as a whole. It shows fragmented thinking, where things fit neatly into little boxes, filed categories, but is far removed from reality where life is lived out in an interconnected way. One cannot keep things separated, or only with dire consequences. The sense of touch and the ego-sense are intimately connected, and as humans we are beings of touch – on a most elemental and primal level. We lose touch or cultivate touch. Without the handshake we are once again contributing more than we might think to the stunting of our senses, to the breakdown of what and who we are as human beings. Through the power of the handshake we are building relationships built on trust – as supported by numerous neuroscientific reports.

Having passed through the gateway of trust, the children enter the classroom.

---

13 Francis Edmunds, *Rudolf Steiner Education: The Waldorf Impulse* (London: Rudolf Steiner Press, 1962), p. 30

14 Rudolf Steiner, *Faculty Meetings with Rudolf Steiner: Volume 2* (Anthroposophic Press, 1998), April 9, 1924

15 Paul Matthews, *Words in Place: Reconnecting with Nature through Creative Writing* (Hawthorn Press, 2007), p. 40

Announcements, Attendance, and Sharing
"Receive the child in reverence, educate the child in love, let the child go forth in freedom"[16]

ONCE INSIDE THE classroom, the rhythm of the daily schedule can commence. Before reciting the Morning Verse with the students, teachers usually take care of some preliminaries, such as announcements and other points of business, which could include reminders about an outing, an assembly, an upcoming parent evening, or anything else that the children need to know. These practical announcements give the late arrivals the chance to get settled in the class. However, they also have a way of usurping precious time. It's best to keep them short and concise, and to refrain from discussing anything that is unnecessary or could be imparted at another time. I have observed classes where the ongoing morning announcements felt like an infringing fog on a clear day.

In the early grades the roll call is often sung using the interval of the fifth: "Matilda (*d*)/ Higgins (up to *a*) / are you (*d*) / here? (*a*)," which then is answered with, "Yes, Mr. (*a*)/ Müller (*d*), /I am (*a*) / here (*d*)."[17] While the fluctuating fifth interval sets a certain calm and flowing mood, I only suggest doing it if it is held in the right spirit by the teacher and does not become an empty or poorly sung routine. The fifth is an interval of balance and breath, so the mood lends itself to early childhood and the first two grades. It is an opportunity to get them to sing the fifths beautifully. However, I have observed teachers who are not able to sing perfect fifths, which, in turn, will be imitated by the children. Instead of fifths, thirds or even minor thirds are sung, which defeats the purpose. Moreover, the starting note is often randomly chosen. The lowest note on the Choroi flute is a "d," so it makes sense to sing the fifth between "d" and "a" because many of the songs they sing will include that range. I have witnessed classes taking up to ten minutes for this due to continuous interruptions. In those cases, it would be better to speak the roll call rather than trying to "force" a properly sung roll call. In short, if sung it should be done fluidly and with conscious intention. When it works it is beautiful and harmonious, and the children experience themselves as beautiful. It is like a musical handshake, an acknowledgement of the child's presence. Some teachers improvise, consciously using different notes of the pentatonic scale, which the children then echo, which fosters listening skills.

Taking attendance, apart from knowing who is present, is a healthy social habit to pursue. The incarnating process raises awareness for one another, thereby instilling a caring atmosphere. We carry the students by acknowledging their presence as well as their absence. In the case of an absent student one can have the entire class sing, "No, Mr. Müller, Justin is not here." In this way the absent child is included in the day's events.

Cultivating healthy habits is a cornerstone of Waldorf education, and it is worthwhile restating its importance. Furthermore, punctuality is a virtue that must and can be fostered, starting with the teacher. Do we start each morning punctually? Are we punctual in our daily lives? Do we arrive at meetings punctually? If we've schooled our own punctuality it will be easier to foster punctuality amongst the students. That does not mean that we need to be dogmatic and disciplinarian about promptness. However, punctuality can be cultivated if it becomes part and parcel of our daily rhythm. As soon as the bell rings the children will automatically line up. Steiner was quite particular about timeliness and addressed it a number of times during the Faculty Meetings.

> When the students are tardy in the morning, it has a bad effect on your teaching. Sometimes when I came here early, I had the impression that the way class was begun in the morning left much to be desired of the teachers. I thought that someone should be in the corridor, so the children wouldn't play hide and seek there.[18]

I have noticed that the teachers who live farthest from the school are often the earliest to arrive, and those who live closest do not necessarily show up on time. For the teacher the old adage rings true: If you arrive early, you are on time. If you are on time, you're late, and if you are late, you're fired. I know of one teacher whose persistent lateness actually did lead to his dismissal. Steiner continues:

> We should be careful that the class teachers do not enter the classroom too late. That is one of the main reasons why the children get into such an uproar, namely that they are left to themselves because the teacher is not there."[19]

Nevertheless, in the early grades it is not always so easy to begin on time. It requires practice. Jackets and coats need to be hung up; indoor shoes need to be put on; children have to use the bathroom; others must be called inside. This can take time. It will fall in place if one works consciously toward punctual beginnings. What tends to happen, however, is that the morning time becomes too loose and children still run around outside even after the bell has rung, or the teacher continues to jump rope with students, or talk to a parent. If parents become accustomed that the Main Lesson only begins about ten or fifteen minutes late, it might lead to them not taking the starting time too seriously. This too needs mindful attention and should be brought up at parent evenings or privately with a parent. In the high school, tardiness is usually not the parents' "fault" anymore, rather an inner lethargy or indifference. I have observed older students casually moseying into the school building with no qualms about arriving late. In the high school it is an ongoing issue that we find ourselves having to discuss periodically.

The tradition of "sharing" in the lower school is sometimes relegated to "circle time," but it can easily be done before the Morning Verse as part of the announcements. In *Practical Advice to Teachers*, Steiner encourages teachers to practice "as much simple speaking and conversation with the children as possible. [...] [W]e start in a small way to let them give brief accounts of experiences they themselves have had. We let the children relate something they like to talk about."[20] This developed over time into a few minutes of *sharing* in the first grade. The best results are achieved if the teacher controls these personal stories. Sharing can be a very useful pedagogical tool. The children practice the retelling of experiences. Free conversation and clear speaking are cultivated. They learn to form their thoughts based on something that has happened in their lives. It is a relaxed and more personal form of recall. They have to search for and find the right words in order to convey their experiences. Giving the children the opportunity to retell their stories, something they feel connected to, will later on give them the needed confidence to talk about academic material linked to the curriculum – the official recall. It encourages them to express their thoughts cogently, and builds a transition from colloquialisms to formal speech.

As they tell their little anecdotes the teacher can gently correct their mistakes in an easygoing and informal manner, their lingering speech error patters (some of them reaching right up into the higher grades), such as "Me and my sister..." instead of "My sister and I." Or if a child says, "I *goed* into the kitchen and saw two *mouses*," you could respond, "Ah, how exciting that you *went* into the kitchen and saw two *mice*." It is very likely that the child will immediately repeat the incident correctly. Depending on the area and the country, the vernacular will be more or less noticeable. Children often don't hear the words correctly, especially when there are regional dialects, even slightest and almost indiscernible changes make a difference ("bin" for "been," or the more obvious colloquialisms such as "gonna" and "wanna" for "going to" and "wanting to").

Sharing is a mild and welcoming way of beginning the day in the early grades, and the children like to share about what the tooth fairy brought, a birthday party they attended, or that their grandparents came to visit. Limits must be set, and the intention behind the sharing should not be forgotten. It's best if each teacher comes up with her or his own guidelines, either choosing a specific number of students who can share, limiting the time, or going by rows, or a combination of the above, depending on the class size. Some topics ought to be strictly off limits, such as discussing movies or talking badly about people. Teachers can also choose themes, such as sharing little stories about their pets, or trips they have gone on, or something they saw on the way to school. Every opportunity to hone their observational skills is educational. Thereby, social lessons are developed. Getting the children to listen to one another or refrain from interrupting, cultivates empathy and consideration for the other person. Through the telling of little stories, the children share something of themselves. They feel heard and seen.

However, if it goes on for too long, then the students will get bored and unruly. As such, the Main Lesson is compromised before it has even begun. If approached correctly, it nurtures interest for life, the other person, and the world. From second grade and up these conversations and exchange of personal news should no longer take up any class time and can easily take place as they enter the classroom first thing in the morning before the start of the Main Lesson, or for special occasions.

---

[16] A quote attributed to Rudolf Steiner, though the reference is not cited. It serves as the unofficial motto of Waldorf Education.

[17] There are numerous variations.

[18] Rudolf Steiner, *Faculty Meetings with Rudolf Steiner: Volume 2*, (Anthropsophic Press, 1998), April 9, 1924, p. 732.

[19] Rudolf Steiner, *Faculty Meetings with Rudolf Steiner: Volume 1* (Anthropsophic Press, 1998) June 17, 1921, p. 279.

[20] Rudolf Steiner, *Practical Advice to Teachers*, (Anthroposophic Press, 2000), Lecture 13, p. 169.

Morning Verse

"Often, when I was by myself, when life's riddles and existential problems weighed me down, my thoughts returned to this verse, and I experienced deeply the great ordering power of these words."[21] Rudolf Grosse

FROM FIRST GRADE through to the senior class Waldorf students recite the Morning Verse written by Rudolf Steiner. There are two: the first verse is recited until the end of 4th grade, and the second verse is for 5th graders and up. It serves as a doorway into the day, a threshold moment before entering into the temple of learning, a centering time of unified focus – the formal beginning of the Main Lesson. It marks a profound moment of the self within the group, the entire school, and the being of the Waldorf movement. Of the many small ceremonious moments within a school day, it is the one that sets the tone for the others yet to come. It is important that all the students be present for the Morning Verse. It does make a difference whether they start the day with or without that verse. A further reason why punctuality should be cultivated. Tardiness too easily becomes a pattern.

Waldorf education promotes healthy habits, embodied through repetition and rhythm. Thus, it serves as a daily foundation for the soul. Schooled habits are grail-like, a living vessel in constant motion, into which learning can flow, held within the embracing movements of the rhythmic rotations. How do we as teachers relate to the respective Morning Verses? How deeply do we connect to them? How important are they to us? To what extent do we meditate on the contents? How do we experience the contents whenever we say the verse? When is the best time to say it? I've seen it said first thing in the morning, and as late as halfway through the main lesson, and sometimes not at all.

On September, 25, 1919 a teacher asked Steiner if it would be good to have a verse to start off the day. Steiner responded positively and immediately, promising to give the teachers an appropriate verse on the following day, which he referred to as the "opening verse." He also strongly cautioned them not to call it a prayer. True to his word he brought and read the two verses to the teachers the very next day, on September, 26, 1919. He suggested they first speak the verse together with the students in chorus, so that the students could live into the tone, tempo and rhythm of the verse, similarly to the way Steiner had read it to the teachers. Only later, once the students would know it by heart, should the teacher offer explanations to the verse's meaning.[22]

Because of its gateway nature it should be well formed and framed. For the early grades many teachers light a beeswax candle and ask the class to stand up to recite the verse. Some teachers also sound a bell, or play a few notes on a chime. I made sure that the children were standing straight and upright. For the first four grades I had them fold their arms across their chests, which is a centering gesture.

> The Sun with loving light
> Makes bright for me each day.
> The soul with spirit power
> Gives strength unto my limbs.
> In sunlight shining clear,
> I reverence, O God,
> The strength of humankind
> Which thou so graciously,
> Has planted in my soul,
> That I with all my might
> May love to work and learn.
> From thee come light and strength,
> To thee rise love and thanks.[23]

This initial coming together as a class through the verse has always felt like a blessing for the day. It exudes warmth, love, and goodness. One can feel held by the gentle positivity of the salutary words. It's a bridge between sleep life and the day's work ahead, between the dark night and the light filled day, between rest and joyous activity. It reminds us from where we have come and what is expected of us. They are like helping hands, pulling us up into uprightness and the abundant possibilities that the day has in store for us. The words are comforting and have a protective and uplifting quality, calling forth the best in us. If held correctly and spoken with the right reverence, the children will experience the "loving light" in themselves, sensing unconsciously that the creative source lives in all people. For the first two grades I added gestures to the words, which I relinquished once we came to third grade, where the children are more earth bound. Steiner even suggested that the verse could be sung, but I have never heard it rendered in song before.

In fifth grade, the so-called "golden year," the students receive the second verse, which will accompany them through high school. By then I no longer required them to fold their arms across their chests, but we would stand upright, arms to the side, come to inner and outer silence, and begin:

I look into the world
In which the sun is shining,
In which the stars are sparkling,
In which the stones repose;
Where living plants are growing,
Where sentient beasts are living,
Where human, soul-gifted, gives
The spirit a dwelling place.

I look into the soul
That lives within my being.
The world-Creator moves
In sunlight and in soul-light,
In wide world space without,
In soul-depths here within.

To Thee, Creator-Spirit,
I will now turn my heart
To ask that strength and blessing
To learn and work may grow
Within my inmost being.

The above translations are by Arvia Mackaye Ege (with slight variations, such as *human*, instead of *man; ask* instead of *beg*), who was one of the founding members of the Hawthorne Valley Waldorf School. There are various translations and it is recommended that the respective schools decide on one translation so that when classes come together, they can recite the same Morning Verse in unison. Some translations are a combination of various translations.

In both verses reverence is paid to the outer world and the inner world. The following well known Steiner quote encapsulates the essence of both verses: "*To truly know the world, look deeply within your own being; to truly know*

yourself, take real interest in the world."[24] It is a theme that
Steiner repeats in different forms over and over again, and
forms the firm foundation of self-knowledge and self-
development. The students feel it, even if they don't always
admit as much.

When my wife entered the 13th grade at the Rudolf
Steiner School in Bochum Langendreer, Germany, to
complete her Abitur, the class decided to still continue
saying the Morning Verse together, though they were no
longer required to do so, which confirms the deep connection
the students had to the Morning Verse.

Similarly, over the last few years when I asked the
seniors whether they still wanted to recite the Morning
Verse during play rehearsals, which always falls at the end
of the school year, they almost always chose to continue,
instead of going with a verse that might lend itself more
specifically to drama.

I work with the verse creatively, not only during the
senior play, but also intermittently during the Main Lessons
in high school, when it can easily turn into empty routine;
when the speech becomes sloppy, or when their physical
heaviness, coupled with morning lethargy, muddies the
words. For example, we have spoken it while some students
improvised gestures or added dance steps. I have encouraged
them to put the verse into their own words. Or we have
thought the verse in silence, sometimes with or without
movements. We have divvied up the lines between the
students, or spoken sections according to rows. We have
whispered the verse, accentuated the rhythms. And in order
to avoid the verse sounding like a dirge we have changed the
pauses to emphasize the meaning. We've spoken the verse in
various languages, which usually gets the students to speak
it with more liveliness. A Chinese student a few years back
brought in a Chinese version. I have asked them what could
take the place of that verse. Though they come up with other
poems, they mostly agree that none of the suggestions is able
to embody the same kind of appropriate and enduring

quality. When I request for volunteers to come to the front and recite the verse by themselves, they often stumble over words, realizing that they have been saying the verse automatically, carried by the group. In the upper grades it is good to wake them up to the words and the meaning, so that they recite the verse more consciously. More often than not it has been the first time that they have knowingly discussed the verse. I have not sung it with them yet, but maybe... next block.

From first grade on I made a point of articulating each word as clearly as possible and imbued the verse with the clarity and musicality of speech. However, I refrained from working on the language in the same rigorous way that I normally did with other poems, preferring to leave it up to them, spurred on by my example. In my first block with the 9th grade, I can ascertain something about the class through the way they recite the Morning Verse. Does it sound like a bored drawl or do they speak out with strength and articulation?

The verse for the upper grades begins with "I," but in many classes that "I" is lost, and students only start speaking on the third or fourth word, because they sheepishly follow the teacher. That too I avoid, asking them to begin consciously with *that special name they collectively call themselves* – the ever elusive "I," the most enigmatic part of themselves, their budding individuality, the spiritual essence of themselves, the captain over their souls. "Put some *will* into it. You owe that to yourselves."

Last year (as of this writing) I received an email from a former student who had graduated the year before, asking for a hard copy of the Morning Verse. Of course, she knew it by heart, but she needed to have the correct punctuation because she wanted to use it for a college paper. The assignment was to write a personal essay based on a piece of literature that has been important to the student. Carly had chosen the Morning Verse. A few weeks later I received the essay, which she'd titled "Sunlight and Soul-Light." She mentions how the verse got so routine during school time that the content of what Steiner wanted to convey got lost. Now that she was in college and "away from the routine" she "wanted to go back and look at the importance of this poem and how it still affects my life." Carly went on to write how it "emphasizes the importance" of every single person. "It expresses how everyone is here on this earth to improve it in some way if they really challenge themselves." She then went into depth, line for line, how it encouraged her to be an *observer* – to truly see the world and the other person, to see and be seen in one's *essence*. She also included a gentle reprimand, how the teachers did not always see her, the struggles she was having. An important reminder: do we see the real inner core of each student? Do we meet them, help them, nurture them, so that they truly feel seen – fully. It made me realize that we teachers are also susceptible to regurgitating the Morning Verse in a dull, desultory manner. Are we thinking about something entirely different while we go through the motions? I have caught myself doing exactly that. (In a recent discussion with my wife, she said that as a student she always thought about the words, every day without fail, right through high school) It was moving to read Carly Disbrow's thoughtful words; how the verse made her want to do her best, and how it continued to support her right through high school. The verse helps "to get you up every morning and to keep your soul and your being growing."

I was struck by a sentence at the end of her essay where she states: "The ending of the poem almost sounds like a *vow*. A vow that is made once you have found your purpose in life."

To ask that strength and blessing
To learn and work may grow
Within my inmost being.

---

[21] Rudolf Grosse, *Erlebte Pädagogik: Schicksal und Geistesweg* (Dornach: Verlag am Goetheanum, 1998), p. 60. (loosely translated by the author). Grosse was a Waldorf Student at the original Waldorf School in Stuttgart and member of the first graduating class. Later her became a Waldorf teacher at the Waldorf School in Basel, Switzerland.

[22] Rudolf Steiner, *Faculty Meetings with Rudolf Steiner: Volume 1*, (Anthroposophic Press, 1998)

[23] Translated by Arvia Mackaye Ege

[24] Rudolf Steiner, *Verses and Mediations* (London: Rudolf Steiner Press, 1979)

Rhythmical Part

"Schooling the senses has become the newest essential for 'truth education.' A major effect of the media has been to attack our ability to school our senses and our ability to find the truth and the good."[25] ~ Michaela Glöckler

THE "OPENING EXERCISES," also referred to as "circle time," usually follows immediately after the Morning Verse and forms the foundational phase of the Main Lesson. I prefer to call it the "rhythmical part" of the morning (from the German – Rhytmischer Teil), because it warmly welcomes the students into the rhythm of the day through the cadences of poetry, music, and movement. Besides, the rhythmical part transcends the scope of mere exercises on a number of levels. Fundamentally, it connects the self to the world with the help all twelve senses (as laid out by Rudolf Steiner), which are addressed and stimulated in one way or other. The senses constitute organs of perception, which need to be furthered and stimulated as much as possible. Especially the fundamental or *will-senses* (movement, balance, touch, and well-being/life), help to awake and quicken the *cognitive senses* (Ego, thought, word, and hearing/sound). And the middle senses (warmth, sight, taste, smell) are primarily concerned with *feeling* (with the sense of warmth and sight reaching up to the higher senses, and taste and smell reaching into the foundational senses). Furthermore, poetry and music not only enrich the true inner soul life, but support the subject matter of the respective blocks to which they are invariably and intimately connected. The Morning Verse is not only the gateway to the day and the Main Lesson, but it inaugurates the rhythmical part, setting it in motion.

The rhythmical part has also received its fair share of negative criticisms in recent years. Though partly justified, it is more a matter of approaching this section with deeper and more artistic insights, rather than devaluing it because it "wastes" valuable time that could be better used for learning. If used correctly it becomes an essential part of learning. The rhythmical part developed naturally and became an integral component of the Main Lesson from the earliest years of Waldorf education. Heinz Müller, who was sent by Rudolf Steiner to teach at the Hamburg Waldorf School in 1923 writes:

> At the beginning of the lesson teacher and children together say a morning-verse. Then there comes some music, with younger children playing block-flutes [recorders] in unison, and later on other instruments as well. As well as this there will be practice in choral singing with instrumental accompaniment. Finally, a series of speech-exercises is done by the children either singly or together, in which the utmost exactitude must be worked for.[26]

The rhythmical part forms the *basis* of the Main Lesson, in that it awakens the "head" forces of the child and tills the soil for cognitive activity. It is no exaggeration to claim that it helps to lay the foundation for culture and civilization. Songs and poems that express natural phenomena artistically and relate to sundry human activities are instilled in the students from early on over many years, with the result that their entire lives are enriched. It heightens their perceptions and naturally draws forth poems or songs that emphasize seasonal qualities: a summer storm, autumnal winds, the gentle falling of snow, a rushing brook, and so forth. For instance, when the first daffodils show themselves in spring, the words, "I wandered lonely as a cloud..." might naturally rise up and turn that moment into a celebration. Inculcated songs and poems grow into lifelong gifts. Waldorf students carry such a treasure trove within them, turning life's prose into poetry.

This section helps to bring the children to their (12) senses. It does not need much to awaken the children, though I am inclined to think that the children nowadays would do well with a *slightly* extended rhythmical part, because poetry, movement, and song are no longer as embedded in our culture so naturally and firmly as in times gone by. Additionally, in this time of screen dominance, our children are deprived of ordered and natural movement like never before in history. We need to reestablish a balance, bringing movement back into the body, soul, and mind. So many children who are *connected* to their screens are *disconnected* from their wills, and in order to wake up in their minds, they first need to be brought into themselves, be "reattached," so to speak. Part of the teacher's responsibility is to gradually bring the developing ego of the child into her or his body, so that they can unfold their individuality. One can call Waldorf education an "ego education" in so far as it makes room for the child to embrace his and her "eternal self" so that in later years, when it grows up, it will be less egoistical. The prerequisite for this is a thorough education of the will, underscored by Willi Aeppli:

Education of the will is impossible without the cultivation of the will-senses. Secondly it is necessary to be aware of the fact, that the proper development of the cognitive senses by which the children learn in school, is bound up with a well-developed will-sense. It is good repeatedly to recall this fact, that the cognitive senses originated through metamorphosis, through a kind of development of the will-senses. A healthy development of the cognitive senses in the child presupposes a healthy lower sense-organism.[27]

On a basic level, the rhythmical part, which addresses the willing and feeling life, attunes and brings the children together, which fosters inner and outer harmony, with the aim of making them more receptive for learning. For the younger grades it can be a bit longer, approximately half an hour to forty-five minutes, and for the later grades it shouldn't extent much beyond fifteen to twenty minutes. If it goes on for too long and is not held properly, then the children will get tired, which leads to disruption. However, the timing depends on the day, the class, the mood, the structure of the morning class, and how the teacher assesses the situation. Another consideration is whether the main lesson lasts a full two hours or only 105 or 90 minutes. Though it has profound pedagogical value, it is *not* meant to be a lesson in singing or movement, but a *warm up,* a *wake up,* albeit a sound and artistically infused warm up with far reaching effects.

Some children need to be roused from their sleepy or sluggish state, while others need to be calmed down. Though Steiner did not explicitly say much about the rhythmical part per se, he repeatedly underscored the practice and importance of poetry and song in the Main Lessons, which was actively taken up by the first Waldorf teachers from 1919 onward. And he often gave teachers movement exercises, sometimes for individual children, but often practiced by the whole class. The intention is to involve the whole child and get them gradually into their will, not through rigorous and mechanical bodily exercises (like gymnastics), but through the implicit rhythms of poetry, music, and formative and harmonizing movements, which stimulates their blood flow and equalizes their breathing.

The teacher can sense at a glance the needs of the class and the individual children. More often than not the students have long commutes, causing them to be either lethargic or hyper. Of course, it makes a difference whether the school is located in a rural, suburban, or urban area. Walking to school would be ideal, but that has become the exception. Mostly they travel by car, bus, subway, or train, where they inevitably are exposed to loud noises, such as traffic or the sound of the car radio. Furthermore, many middle and high school students are hooked to their gadgets, closed off to the outer world and listening to music through their ear buds. And how many have had breakfast? Fortunately, the combination of speech, singing, flute or recorder playing, concentration exercises, and finger and movement games, can harmonize the children and bring a semblance of order and balance into their potentially hectic mornings.

It is, however, important that this rhythmical section in the morning does not become a routine, enacted in a perfunctory manner. It needs to remain alive based on clear expectations. It is not a matter of spending too much time on these opening activities, but the time must be well used, which means that the rhythmical part needs to proceed in a focused, orderly, and artistic manner. The poems and songs bring joy into the morning, thereby unifying the class. Once they are brought together and woken up, they are ready to receive and absorb the contents of the lesson.

Apart from harmonizing their breathing and blood circulation, this rhythmic work will improve their skills. It strengthens them as a group and individually. It also offers many opportunities for the teacher to observe the students as they grapple and cope with the various activities – nimbleness of body and mind, ability to focus, elasticity of speech, and so forth. Although imitation still plays a strong role in the first and second grade, one should aim to have them speak, sing, and play, without the support of the teacher.

When the child enters the classroom, it carries with it the echoes of sleep life. The body, though still gradually waking up, has rested and been rejuvenated. And according to the teachings of Pythagoras, the world of sleep is infused with cosmic music, where the fixed stars, sun, moon, and planets have their unique voices, singing together in a mighty ever-changing chorus: the "music of the spheres." Plato alludes to it, and Aristotle cogently expounds on Pythagoras's harmony of the spheres. Rudolf Steiner, using theosophical terms, talks about the realm of *devachan* through which we traverse every time we go to sleep. The lower devachan is silent and is filled with moving color. As we enter the higher devachan we begin to hear sound. The harmony of the spheres fills out the flowing world of color, and in the highest part of devachan we hear the musically infused spoken word – the *logos*.[28] As Pythagoras taught his students in his mystery school in Croton, southern Italy, the sounding harmonies grow fainter as we approach and are drawn back to earth from the vastness of the sounding cosmos, until we are left with silence and darkness. He was speaking from direct experience. Yet, we all have a faint memory of these celestial harmonies, and the creation myths from around the world allude to this divine music. It is the reason why we love music so much. It reminds us of devachan. With this in mind we can understand the wisdom of starting the school day with poetry and music, for it reminds the children from where they have come, their *true home*. Through music, speech, and movement we remember the rhythms of the cosmos, the sounds and rhythms of the supersensible symphony.

Other activities, such as mental math exercises, have become a staple during the rhythmical part. They can be practiced in various forms, which help to address different modalities of learning. For the more auditory students one can use sounds to represent numbers: for example: a chime for the digits, a bell for the tens, and a drum for the hundreds, or the rhythmic practicing of the tables with clapping, bean bags, or lummi sticks. There are endless possibilities: the use of hand gestures, bodily movements, ball throwing, or simply going through a number story. In between it is advisable to give these exercises a rest, letting them sink in, in order to wake them up again at a later time in a slightly changed form. And some teachers forego these exercises while they are in a math block.

The wisdom of starting the school day with poetry, song, and games is something I can only confirm and acknowledge with the utmost enthusiasm. After more than three decades of teaching I have experienced the valuable and health-giving effects first hand. The rhythmical part has been essential to my Main Lessons throughout the grades, including in the high school, though it takes on a different form and is much reduced. It is an integral part of the morning. It sets, stabilizes, and reinforces the mood. It is like the heavenly whiff of freshly baked bread – food for the soul. Above all, it's enjoyable.

SPEECH

"Today the original impulse of speech is present in [human] *kind only in the very smallest degree. There is ample reason for the fact. Unhappily, speech as an art has no place now in education. In our schools, and the schools of other nations too, have lost touch with art altogether; and that is why in our Waldorf School we have to make such a strong stand for the artistic in education."*[29] Rudolf Steiner

DURING STEINER'S "discussions" with the founding teachers of the Waldorf School he noticed that their articulation and capacities for rich and living narrative needed work. He first brought it up in the 4th *Discussion* and arrived with freshly penned speech exercises the very next day (August 26. 1919). "I should like you to pass these sentences round and repeat them in turn without embarrassment so that by constant practice they may make our speech organs elastic; we can make these organs do gymnastics as it were. Frau Steiner will say the sentences first as it should be done artistically, and I will ask each one of you to repeat them after her."[30]

From then on, each *Discussion* began with speech exercises, a mini "rhythmical part" for the teachers. And teachers need rhythmical awakening in speech and music just as much as do the children, if not more. After all, the teacher's greatest tool is her or his voice, most importantly in the second seven-year cycle of the growing child, where the teaching is predominantly in narrative, and where the child has a hunger for all that is pictorial. Or in in Steiner's words: "Cultivate speech in yourself and your children with the greatest care, since far and away the most of what a teacher gives [her or] his children comes to them on the wings of speech."[31] Speech not only conjures forth the imaginations but fills the pictures with refinement of soul, especially in all that is moral in the language.[32] The speech of the teacher has immense significance, and it demands constant practice. This is even more true for the early grades, where the children, still living in the echo of imitation, and are physically affected by their teacher's speech patterns, the dynamics and inflections.

"In the beginning was the word," is monumentally stated at the beginning of St. John's Gospel. It always has been and always will be. In speech we recognize "a relationship between the human being and the cosmos."[33] Practicing speech and entering into great poetry from the very first day of grade one is a way of latching on to this sacred and primal force, imbued by the divine spark, especially in our age where speech has been impoverished and reduced to such a shocking degree, helped along by the digital tsunami. Speech has to a large degree lost its place in the seven liberal arts

and needs to be reinstated, resuscitated, renewed. Students enter school with any number of speech defects that need conscious attention. And even when there are no speech defects, we notice slovenly, muddy, and inarticulate speech, which then becomes the norm. The correct formation of speech is the foundation of good grammar and spelling (including the vagaries of phonics), and serves as a prerequisite for clear thinking. It lifts the mood, oxygenates the blood and is a creative force – as is music and the arts as such.

In little infants, speech is developed out of movement and it precedes thinking. It is always a wonder how quickly the children learn to speak their mother tongue, and it is all through *imitation*. Therefore, it behooves the adults around the children to always speak as clearly and as beautifully as possible. Telling stories and reading to them is invaluable and can never really be made up later in life. In the first two grades imitation is still markedly strong – a carry-over from the first seven years. Therefore, the teacher's speech is of greatest importance. At the same time, the children have entered the second seven-year cycle where they learn the content of the lessons through strong imaginations given to them by a person who they love and revere – a benevolent and trusted *authority* figure.

Tongue twisters and age appropriate vocal drills precede the poems, which warm up and loosen the muscles of the mouth. Rhythm is the foundation of all poetry, especially true for the young child, which makes it so effective. Already with first graders one can work on the speech quite thoroughly, and one should not rely solely on their capacities of imitation. It's good to develop the habit of having them listen to the quality of their own speech. Are they speaking together in unison? Are the consonants clearly articulated? Are the vowels broadened and filled out? Can they develop flexibility so that they can say *"Red leather, yellow leather"* speedily five times in a row? (Some students might still be saying "lellow" for yellow.) Even in the first or second grade one can ask for "brave volunteers" to speak the tongue twisters singly. It usually brings mirth into the classroom, whether it is in the first grade or in the senior class. Many of the speech exercises for first grade I wrote myself, based on the letters of the alphabet, one for each letter: "*The wild waves had whisked / And washed the wide ships / Onto the white beach where the / Weary men now slept / Under a weeping willow.*"[34] In this example, we can see how it clearly relates to the Main Lesson block on writing.

As for the poetry: though one chooses age appropriate poems, there is no need to choose simple and superficial poems for the young ones. The language is what is important – the rhythm, rhyme, and sounds of the words! The Morning Verse, for example, is poetic and deeply meaningful. Poems should be chosen for their artistic merit as much as for their content. The children do not necessarily need to understand the poems in an analytical manner, but can enjoy their musicality and the mood they convey. However, one should not forget to introduce these poems with imaginative pictures and some explanations that bring them into context, that helps the children understand the essence of the poems, and why they were chosen – a point of orientation. In the early grades the children yearn to add gestures to the words, to walk the rhythms of the poems, to sense the syllables in their arms, hands and fingers. They can almost taste the language through the movement. Certain combination of sounds, which appeal to them, they love to repeat over and over again. Care must be taken that the gestures remain in the service of the language, of the poetry. Instinctual movements, as with sports, should be avoided. The movements help the articulation, but should not be too limp and light, nor too hard and loud. As in so much in life – balance is the key.

After the nine-ten-year change, one can gradually diminish the bodily movements and focus purely on the language, the dynamics, the phrasing, and the subtleties. Choric speaking nourishes the soul life of the students right through the grades. Rhythm lives in the heart, and the heart never sleeps, never tires, and in that sense, we latch on to the heart forces. It does not need much to see the color come into their faces, and to see them refreshed and ready to learn and listen.

Over the years the students who have gone through Waldorf School have a whole treasury of poetry stored within them. Those with a good memory will be able to recite them throughout their lives. My wife, for instance, will suddenly recite a poem or sing a song, prodded by a memory, the season, a sun or moonrise, morning mist, the mention of a name – anything. I am always in awe at what sometimes comes forth that has been dormant, sometimes for decades. And that is also true for my three sons who went through Waldorf, although they don't express it quite so freely.

MUSIC

"In the course of humanity's historical evolution, speech has emerged from a primeval song element. The further we go back into prehistoric times, the more speech resembles recitation, and finally singing."[35] ~ Rudolf Steiner

TO BE GIVEN THE chance to sing every day – what a gift! In cultures all around the world, dancing and singing was embedded in the daily rhythms of people, from dawn to dusk, and often deep into the night. It was a given. Almost every task was accompanied by a song, turning a chore into joy, transmuting rote into ritual, letting eternity glow and gleam from within the moment. The greater the pity that in our modern cultures it is no longer necessarily so – not in most homes, nor in many schools, let alone the workplace. There is no guarantee that children will even receive rudimentary music classes. Of course, chorus and "band" are still offered, and maybe the school even has an orchestra, but it is generally only available to middle or high school students or those who choose to sing or play an instrument, which could lead to a form of discriminating between those who are talented and the others.

When I ask the students in our teacher education classes what their musical experiences were like at school, I am repeatedly astounded to hear how rarely they sang in school or elsewhere. It has become the exception for students to be versed in basic music literacy (and I am not referring to trained musicians). Most do not know the difference between a whole tone and a half tone (let alone the difference between a crotchet and a quaver), major and minor, or the meaning of an interval. Not only do they feel that they missed out on something integral, but they are deeply saddened that they received so little music while growing up. One only has to listen to a group of people singing "Happy Birthday" to note how even the simplest of melodies are sung out of tune. Yet, singing alone or together with others belongs to one of the most enjoyable pastimes for children and adults alike. It unites people, it heightens the moment, it is celebratory. Singing is a social deed, par excellence. It's quintessentially human. But if it has been denied or deemed unimportant, then the children, and later the adults, will automatically shy away from music and rarely pursue it on their own accord, leaving the soul undernourished. There is truth to the words of Reinhild Brass, longtime music teacher at the Widarschule in Wattenscheid: "When the musician within the human being falls ill, is stunted or even dies, then, essentially, the whole human being dies."[36] No wonder then, that our present time is beset by seemingly insurmountable problems: pandemics, wars, greed, power struggles, the endangered environment. Society needs, like never before, the harmonizing effects of music. Music helps to consolidate the etheric life forces to the physical body, which, in turn, will make us more effective in the world.

Humans inherently have a deep yearning for music and are grateful for any opportunity, should they arise. We are all intrinsically musical, though it embodies itself differently in people. The teacher education students are therefore thankful to receive some experience of music in our program, though it is never enough. However, for many of them, as is true for numerous adults, participating in music is often coupled with a sense of shame, even dread; a fear of being laid bare, of not singing correctly – the sound of one's own voice. They feel exposed. Music illiteracy abounds, and even singing by ear and holding a tune is no longer self-evident. All the more reason to create a safe place for the inner musician to develop. Every sound shapes us, just as every sense perception has formative effects, especially on the very young child.

Having direct musical experiences is not only a human right, but it belongs to the essential necessities of life, vital to any education. The soul needs musical nurturing in order to reach its full potential. As the Bard said in *Twelfth Night*, "If music be the food of love; play on." And all learning should be based on love. And that is why singing is included in the Main Lessons from first grade through 8th grade, and ideally in the high school classes as well. Like speech, it unifies and sets the mood. And indeed, in most Waldorf classes, even outside Main Lesson, singing or some musical element is included, especially during the foreign languages, eurythmy, and, of course, in the music classes. But songs can also introduce painting or drawing classes, handwork and woodwork classes. Music is alive and well in Waldorf Schools.

For the first two grades Rudolf Steiner suggested that the singing of pentatonic songs, based on the fifth interval, lend themselves most intimately to this age group. His indications were subsequently taken up and thoroughly explored and developed. What has come to be known as "the mood of the fifth" is now practiced in Waldorf Schools around the world: music that is not yet weighed down by the tonic of tonality. As we know, when playing the black keys of the piano, none of the notes will sound "wrong," and we can end the tune on any note. It will always sound fine and will not clamor for a resolution.

The 5th interval is an open interval that hovers around the edges of our bodies. It is an interval of balance. The rising and descending fifth takes us slightly out of and slightly into our bodies, not too much and not too little. In that sense we can also call it the interval of breath: a gentle and calming in and out breath. The mood of the fifth supports and melds with the feeling of wonder that one finds in fairytales – free of the limits of time and space. As the old adage goes: "All learning begins with wonder." The mood of the fifth is not so earth bound and, as mentioned, has a loose connection to time and space, just like the children in the first two grades. It facilitates gentle incarnation.

The songs mostly relate to the seasons and to the respective curriculum. Yet, the mood of the fifth is *not so easy for most people to understand.* For many teachers (even musicians) it takes a while to live into their timeless mood, and to discover their magic. Some teachers even feel a resistance to them. But if one takes the needed time to uncover their essence one will experience their salutary effects, or in the words of Nancy Blanning in the Foreword to the book *The Mood of the Fifth*, "If we can deepen our understanding of this music, cultivate it within our own souls, and practice it every day, this potentized song can reach every child in every class as a healing balm."[37] During my Waldorf practicum at the Widarschule in Wattenscheid, Germany, I was lucky enough to be fully immersed in the mood of the fifth. At that school they had introduced music as a Main Lesson subject (which I have not encountered in any other school since then). At that time, I did not know about the theoretical background of this "new music." But I experienced its effects and kept wondering what made this music *feel* so different. What gives it that pure airy atmosphere? How can it conjure up this unique mood? It made perfect sense, however, when Reinhild Brass explained it to me. I arrived at an immediate understanding because I had experienced it intimately and could observe directly how the children responded to the hovering tonal quality and "open" mood of this music.

The implementation of the "mood of the fifth" now also belongs to the foundational features of Waldorf Schools. The mood of the fifth, of course, is not only dependent on the pentatonic scale, but also in the soft and light manner of singing, according to the rhythm of the breath. The songs do not emphasize the rhythm of the pulse, let alone the beat. That said, one can enjoy the rhythmic element and also include simple diatonic folk songs. But, if one does not cultivate the mood of the fifth, at least to some degree, then the children are missing out on an artistic and soul nurturing element that they will never again be able to recoup at a later stage with the same wholesome effects. They will have missed out on something that can never be reclaimed. I mention this because, like some of the other "Waldorf fundamentals," it is also at risk of being neglected, overlooked, misunderstood, and discarded.

With every grade the songs become ever more challenging. Diatonic songs are predominantly sung in the third grade, with the aim of singing together in unison. Once they have learned to sing together with clarity and confidence, they are ready to sing rounds, usually in 4th grade, though some classes might be ready at the end of 3rd grade (it's advisable to resist the temptation to sing rounds too early). From fifth grade onward, the children will be exposed to part singing with the result that the students will be able to sing complex music from the classical repertoire as well as diverse vocal music from around the world, often coupled with attendant folk dances.

All the students learn how to play an instrument, starting in first grade. In the first two grades, the Choroi pentatonic flutes are used, because of their soft, mellow tone. They blend beautifully with the children's voices and are in concordance with the mood of the fifth. It is usually introduced by the class teacher during the Main Lesson. Many teachers wait until after the break in January to introduce the flutes. However, I suggest introducing them within the first four weeks of school so that they can get used to them and practice their fine motor skills in the process. Furthermore, I recommend using the Choroi flutes over other pentatonic flutes that have come onto the market. As yet, none can compare to Choroi's softness and lightness of tone.

The soprano recorders are introduced in 3rd grade, though often the Choroi soprano flutes are used in 3rd and 4th grade as a natural transition to the recorders. In 5th grade one can introduce the alto recorder, and for the middle school the tenor recorder. For some students in 8th grade, those with big hands and long fingers, one can even bring out the bass recorder. This allows for wonderful four-part harmonies. If the ensemble plays well it can sound almost like an organ.

To underscore: playing recorders and singing during this part of the main lesson must not be confused with a music class. However, it serves as a huge support to the music teacher. Because there are usually only one or two music lessons a week, the main lesson offers a few welcome minutes to practice the music and solidify what has been introduced in the music classes (and vice versa). And it does

not need much. A few songs will suffice. And with the flute
and recorder playing one can alternate the days when one
sings or practices instrumental music. In many cases the
students will play the songs they sing on the recorder as well,
which also helps to work economically with time. If the class
teacher feels insecure in the realm of music, then the music
teacher is usually more than willing to come into class for a
few minutes during specific Main Lessons to work on songs,
Choroi flutes, or recorder playing.

CIRCLE TIME

*"I found that the time devoted to our circle actually enabled
us to learn in a far more economical way than if we had
skipped it: circle time made us more efficient. The children
retained more because they were active in the learning
process."*[38] ~ Torin M. Finser

CIRCLE TIME HAS become a staple morning activity. It
was inevitable that it would develop, because the circle is
part and parcel of so many *movement* exercises and games,
which are usually accompanied by songs or poems. The huge
class sizes in the original Stuttgart school and the relatively
small classrooms made it difficult to create a circle. The class
I attended for a year in Stuttgart had had over 40 students
since 1st grade and the desks were crammed together. And
managing a circle with so many students is cumbersome to
say the least. It developed naturally, especially in the schools
with smaller class sizes, as was the case in England. Circles
could be formed in seconds with no trouble at all. But
currently, with the innovation and steady spread of the
"movable classroom" in Waldorf schools, the furniture can
now be easily moved and is no longer such an impediment,
even for large classes. It's interesting to note that the
movable classroom was developed in Germany because it

was recognized that there needed to be more movement in the Main Lessons, especially in the lower grades.

I made much use of "circle" time during the first three grades, and some of 4th grade. In fifth grade when my class grew to 26 students, I reduced it considerably, nor was it as fitting and necessary anymore as we were transitioning into the middle grades.

Apart from getting the young children out from behind their desks and moving, the ordered movement educates community building, healthy social interaction, and group work. The children see each other in a different context and learn to accept each other's strengths and weaknesses. There are *listening* games of a more musical nature, which can be expanded upon during the music classes; movement games that feed into the PE classes; concentration games that support eurythmy, and a whole array of bean bag exercises that aid the times tables and number work. Looking at the present circumstances, and looking toward the future, it is evident that the child is in more need of formative movements than in previous generations, especially with the inundation of passive media exposure, where even the youngest of children are using smart phones, iPads, and other devices. Healthy outdoor activities are no longer a given. Even riding a bicycle is foreign to many students.

The children enjoy these activities immensely. It brings pleasure, excitement, and wakefulness into the morning, and it makes a change from all the *frontal* learning. On a cautionary note: the circle games should also be limited. The music classes, games, physical education, and eurythmy classes will expand on them later on during the day. We have to remind ourselves that the rhythmical part attunes and wakes the children up, readying them for receptive learning. Circle time is not meant to tire them out. Besides, movement exercises are will exercises, and the will lives in the unconscious, not in the waking consciousness, though they are linked to the cognitive sense of the word. Simply doing random movements makes us tired, and that is why it is advantageous to connect the movements to the rhythms of speech or song, because then we include the rhythmic system, which never tires. We only need to think of the rhythmic pulse of the heart and the steady breath. For these morning movement exercises we want the children to enter into their bodies, reaching down to their toes and out to their fingertips, soulfully. Nimble bodies make nimble minds.

To underscore: the main emphasis of the rhythmical part is to harmonize the students, getting them receptive and ready for the formal and academic part of the lesson. Some teachers have preferred to include the rhythmical part later on in the morning, between the presentation of the new material and the bookwork. At times I have also found it helpful to approach the Main Lesson structure in different ways. Of ongoing importance, however, is that these activities remain fresh, joyous and uplifting. It is a true treat to walk through any Waldorf school in the early mornings and to hear the hallways resound with choral speech, song, instruments, clapping, stamping, and other intriguing sounds. Without doubt, these happy emanations from the various classrooms are health-giving in body, soul, and mind

[25] Michaela Glöckler, *Truth, Beauty and Goodness: The future of education, healing arts and health care* (Hudson, NY: Waldorf Publications, 2019), p. 11

[26] Heinz Müller, *Healing Forces in the Word and its Rhythms: Report Verses in Rudolf Steiner's Art of Education* (Forest Row: Rudolf Steiner Schools Fellowship Publications, 1983), p. 13.

[27] Willi Aeppli, *The Care and Development of the Human Senses* (Forest Row: Steiner Schools Fellowship Publications, 1993).

[28] Rudolf Steiner, *The Inner Nature of Music and the Experience of Tone,* Lecture II (Spring Valley, NY: Anthroposophic Press, 1983).

[29] Rudolf Steiner, *Speech and Drama* (Spring Valley: Anthroposophic Press, 1986), Lecture 1, September 5, 1924, p. 29

[30] Rudolf Steiner, *Discussions with Teachers* (London: Rudolf Steiner Press, 1967), p. 53

[31] Rudolf Steiner, *Speech and Drama* (Spring Valley: Anthroposophic Press, 1986) September 1924

[32] Rudolf Steiner, *Human Values in Education,* (Great Barrington: Anthroposophic Press, 2004), Lecure 3, Arnheim, July 19, 1924.

[33] Rudolf Steiner, *Practical Advice to Teachers,* (Great Barrington: Anthroposophic Press, 2000), p. 24.

[34] Eric G. Müller, *Life Poems for My Students: Birthday and other Verses* (Alkion Press, 2016), p. 87.

[35] Rudolf Steiner, *The Inner Nature of Music and the Experience of Tone* (Anthroposophic Press, 1983), p. 32.

[36] Reinhild Brass, „Schöpferisches Musizieren – Musik in der Widarschule," trans. Eric G. Müller, in *Erziehen und Heilen durch Musik,* (Hrsg.) Gerhard Beilharz (Stuttgart: Verlag Freies Geistesleben, 1989), p. 144.

[37] Nancy Blanning, "Foreword," in *The Mood of the Fifth: A Musical Approach to Early Childhood,* ed. Nancy Foster (Spring Valley: WECAN, 2013), p. IX.

[38] Torin M. Finser, *School as a Journey: The Eight-Year Odyssey of a Waldorf Teacher and his Class,* (Anthroposophic Press, 1994), p. 31.

Report Verses

"Then we agree that we will do the reports as we did last year. Give as true a picture as possible. At the bottom of each report, write a verse for each child that expresses the child's individuality, that can act as a leitmotif for the future."[39] ~ Rudolf Steiner

IN LOWER SCHOOL, after the rhythmical part (some teachers prefer having the children recite the report verses after the Morning Verse), I had the respective children come to the front of the class to recite their *report verses*, also called birthday verses. Rudolf Steiner recommended that the class teachers write a verse for each student at the end of their reports, which would serve as an artistic summation of the year's work. It was suggested that this verse should be recited once a week during the following year. It has been argued that they waste time, especially in big classes, and that the children lose interest and get bored. Indeed, if the verses are not held in the right spirit, then it is best to let it be, but that holds true for everything else we do in the class, including the Morning Verse. I consider the report verses as belonging to the so called "Waldorf fundamentals," alongside eurythmy, the Main Lesson, form drawing, not giving grades (in the lower school), and the role of the class teacher. That the "report verses" are now questioned and being partially discarded, makes for a timely opportunity to reexamine them anew. Instead of disregarding these "Waldorf essentials," we should rather ask ourselves *why* Rudolf Steiner considered them as pedagogically essential in the first place.

Writing these verses sometimes took me more time than the actual report. It was an opportunity to live fully into the child, bring them before my inner eye, and connect with their being. Sometimes it took me days until I had chosen the theme that would be appropriate for the student. During that creative task I often had the feeling that something ineffable and inexplicable was entering the poems. I did not take this task lightly, especially considering that the children would be reciting their respective verses throughout the following year once a week. Each verse needed to contain a universal element that would transcend time and not have lost its meaning for the child after a few months. Furthermore, it should have something that would be soul nourishment for all the students, because they get to listen to every poem once a week for a year. They strengthen the inner contact between the students. These medicinal verses have a marked homeopathic moral effect.

This tradition is being lost in many Waldorf Schools. In some cases, they have been relegated to the realm of "Waldorf myths" and discontinued. The practice has been so neglected that many teachers have not even heard about report verses and the important role they played in Waldorf Schools. Yet, Steiner was ardent that they be written. At best, some teachers give their students a verse on their birthdays, without requiring weekly recitation, with the result that the "birthday verse" becomes another example of Waldorf ephemera. It is not enough to give the students a verse that they only hear or read once. The verses need to be spoken again and again if there is to be any therapeutic or healing effect.

I have never experienced the poems as a waste of time, nor did it ever take up that much time, even when I had well over twenty students in my class. With about five students a day it only took a few minutes. One can also write short verses, which only take a few seconds to recite. The content of the verses is often based on the previous year's curriculum, thus also serving as a reminder of what has been covered in the past. Some teachers might feel they don't have the poetic expertise to write the verses. To those teachers Steiner recommended that they should just try again, and that they would eventually get it right. Admittedly, it is time consuming to write them, which is why teachers often choose verses from other authors. That already happened when

Steiner was alive. Speaking and hearing an array of pithy poems or sayings over many years adds up to quite a commendable literary body of knowledge.

Heinz Müller, who pioneered the Hamburg Waldorf School in Steiner's time, and who received private speech instruction from Steiner, writes about the report-verses in his book *Healing Forces in the Word and its Rhythms*: "I so arranged it that every child said its verse on the day of the week on which it was born, with the Sunday children leading off on Monday mornings."[40] And a bit further on Heniz Müller observes that there were often "remarkable karmic correspondences [that] showed themselves in the groups arising in this way out of the weekdays of birth."[41] This is possibly the reason why these verses are also called birthday verses. On the actual birthday of a student, I had the rest of the class recite the verse for the birthday child. It struck me how well the others could speak the verse of each student, though we never practiced the verse in unison. Thus, every child got to know the verses of their classmates.

In our school in Eugene we handed out the reports on the last day of school. It was a ceremonious event. I made a point of reading the verses to my students, without letting them know who it was for. The students, however, always knew, guessing correctly almost every time. They experienced the poems like a gift, feeling appreciated and supported through the verses.

It has been revelatory to me to note how these words have helped to strengthen and encourage the students. Comparing, contrasting, and compiling the verses many years later, I noticed recurring themes, which goes to show that some challenges take years to overcome, and need to be stated again in different ways. Some proved prophetic, and indeed, Heinz Müller mentions that Steiner wanted the teachers to develop a sense akin to "true prophets." The report verse I wrote for one student in third grade was titled "Master Builder." Now he is a successful architect. For another girl who loved to linger in the paradisiacal world for as long as possible I wrote a poem that I hoped would ease the burden of being "cast out of Paradise" in third grade. To offer strength and to soften the painful feeling of separation between herself and the world I wrote "I Lift my Hands." Here is an excerpt:

> Now I have awoken from my dream,
> And I am here and the world is there.
> I lift my hands into the air,
> Ready for the work that needs to be done.[42]

She became more active in the outer world than I could ever have imagined, honing her skills, and delving fully into all forms of practical work. Already in high school she joined a Search and Rescue team as a volunteer, and later on became a policewoman. After many years she bought a farm in Idaho, where she is cultivating her own paradise on earth.

For another student who had excess energy and carried some unresolved anger within him, I wrote verses that had to do with storm clouds, "dark and threatening," or featured the mythic hero Hercules, who had to learn how to control his strength. Later on in life, this particular student had a tragic and almost fatal snowboarding accident that forced him to slow down, after which he studied art and became a social activist.

These are just three examples of many, and many Waldorf teachers have similar stories. While compiling a book on these report-verses I was moved, again and again, how future bearing they proved to be. Steiner wanted these verses to be like an inner guiding star, which would address some remedial needs.

In 1924 Rudolf Steiner again comes to talk about the report verses in his last lecture on education in Torquay, England. The only slight difference is that this time he suggests putting the verse at the beginning of the report:

> And then every year each child receives in the report
> a personal motto or verse, which can be a word of

guidance in the year to come. The report is like this: first there is the child's name and then the verse, and then the teacher – without using stereotyped letters or numbers [grades] – simply characterizes what the child is like, and what progress she or he has made in the different subjects. [...] The children always love their reports, and their parents also get a true picture of what the child is like at school."[43]

In the original German Steiner refers to the "verses" as *Lebenssprüche*, which translates more correctly as *life-verses* or *life-poems*. May Waldorf schools once again take up this worthwhile endeavor or continue to deepen and spread this valuable impulse.

[39] Rudolf Steiner, *Faculty Meetings with Rudolf Steiner: Volume 1* (Anthroposophic Press, 1998), 5. 26. 1921, p. 252.

[40] Heinz Müller, *Healing Forces in the Word and its Rhythms: Report Verses in Rudolf Steiner's Art of Education* (Forest Row: Rudolf Steiner Schools Fellowship Publications, 1983), p. 13.

[41] Ibid.

[42] Eric G. Müller, *Life Poems for My Students: Birthday and other Verses* (Alkion Press, 2016), p. 39.

[43] Rudolf Steiner, *The Kingdom of Childhood* (Anthroposophic Press, 1995), Lecture 7, p. 123.

Review

"Everything depends on what passes into the subconscious in a way that enables it to be recalled. The subconscious belongs to our being as much as the conscious. In all these matters, we must realize that the purpose of education is to appeal both to the whole person and to that individual's various members."[44] ~ Rudolf Steiner

THE REVIEW OR recall brings to consciousness the previous day's work and, as such, addresses the head forces, the thinking capacity. Though recognized as an important part of the Main Lesson, it can be enhanced and deepened with mindful direction. One has to take care not to put too much emphasis on mere recollection of the story or subject matter, based on questions and answers. It is not meant to be an intellectual exercise that tests students' memory. On the contrary, we want to engage them all in a lively and imaginative manner, not only those who can remember details effortlessly. Steiner, though not averse to the retelling of stories, found it less important, for "indeed, it is not so essential that the children should hold such a story in their memory; in fact [...] this hardly comes into question at all [...] for what has been forgotten is of no consequence."[45] (He is speaking about children between first and fourth grade.) He adds, almost slyly, that if the children are asked to retell the story, the teacher should first say something about the story, "either cleverly or foolishly."

The aim, rather, is to have them to relive the story of the previous day's lesson, but with an *added gleam* that strengthens the moral foundation. The review has distinct components, and, depending on the block, the age group, and the students' engagement, the emphasis might shift.

Of utmost importance is that the students have had the chance to sleep over the material presented to them. For a Waldorf teacher the night plays a significant role. It's like taking the kneaded dough that has been carefully prepared during the Main Lesson and allowed to rise overnight. In other words, while their physical and etheric bodies are resting and rejuvenating, the astral bodies and egos enter into the starry worlds of the hierarchies, taking the soul-experiences and the events of the day with them. If the substance of the lessons was artistically presented, meaningfully developed, and imbued with spirit, it will serve as sustenance for the hierarchies, and they, in turn, can reinforce the content within the children, so that the transformed experiences are imprinted more firmly into their etheric and physical bodies when they wake up in the morning. Consequently, they have gained a deeper and more personal understanding of what they received. Over time these "coagulated" experiences strengthen faculties and develop character. During this segment of the Main Lesson the students will subsequently re-*call,* re-*view* and re-*live,* the contents with added insights, having made it more their own. The ideal of this re-*membering,* is to incorporate the *whole* child in this awakening process – all the various members that make up the human being.

To avoid intellectual regurgitation, it helps to connect the students with something that they can identify with, individually and as a group. If, for example they heard a story of a brave girl entering a forest alone where wild animals roam, you could ask the class whether they would have had the courage to do what the girl did? At that moment you might look at the choleric child. Or if you are reviewing an episode from *The Adventures of Strong Vanya* by Ottfried Preussler, you could ask what it must have been like lying on top of the large oven for seven years doing nothing, just waiting to gain strength. This time you might look over at the phlegmatics, who would have a good understanding of that. Out of such a question, other aspects of the story might be recalled more easily, without necessarily having to ask any further questions.

During the review they are individually re-experiencing the content that has now imprinted itself more firmly within them. This heightened consciousness gives them the opportunity to ponder the material more objectively, forming their own judgments and arriving at their own conclusions. Reconnecting to the content with their feelings will give rise to an opinion, even if it shifts in the course of time.

Recall is a bit like a group of friends getting together and talking about a common experience. Apart from reliving the shared moments, we usually add what that moment meant for us. There is a qualitative enhancement of the occurrence – a new understanding. One gains different perspectives, as well as bolstering the feelings connected to the material. The review is like a second coat of paint, or – to add onto a previous image – like dough transformed to bread. If the review goes well it truly is like "breaking bread."

However, there is also the danger of letting the review go on for too long, where it hemorrhages into mere sharing of stories, which only vaguely relate to the actual lesson material, where one thing leads randomly to another, ending up taking the place of the lesson. The review, like anything else, must remain well guided, and care must be taken that the valuable time does not get usurped by a few students who are excitedly telling their stories, while others are getting increasingly restless, dreamy, or bored, which spoils the mood and wastes time. On the other hand, the review is sometimes skipped over entirely, with no connection made to the previous day, or only addressed in passing. In both cases, profound opportunities are missed.

During the review the quiet and introverted students must not be overlooked, which easily happens. More often than not, a lot is going on within them, but it is helpful, both for them and the class, to have those reticent students share some of their thoughts, which often yield surprising results, stimulating further conversation. I see this particularly in the high school. Often, they really want to, but are too shy or reserved. That's when one can say, "I see that you have a good thought. Let's hear it?" Others may worry that they will say something that might be construed as stupid. On no account should one put anyone on the spot. It's a matter of drawing them out.

On a purely practical level, other aspects of the previous day's lesson can be added to fill out the picture. It is a fact that one frequently forgets relevant and important details, and the review gives one a second chance to weave in essential information. This too will inevitably add time to the review, but it is one area that I have allowed myself to be flexible, though it should not take the place of the new material.

The review offers a time to recapitulate and summarize the essence of the lesson in a logical manner, especially at the end of a section, such as passing from acoustics to optics in a physics block, where one might also read over the observations and conclusions written up over the last few days, either together from the board, or listening to individual students read drafts of their observations (or essays).

Key questions that I like to ask the students at the end of the previous day's presentation can also serve as a stimulus to the review. Sometimes I encourage them to talk to their parents regarding a certain topic. For example, when covering the Voyages of Discovery in 7th grade, you might urge them ask their parents if they have ever gone on an adventure or a voyage of exploration to discover something new and different. It includes the parents in the education of the child, something which Steiner enthusiastically encouraged: "You really must say things to the children that they will want to tell their parents at the next meal. And if you succeed in interesting them [...], you really have carried off the prize."[46] It is a form of homework.

One central purpose of the review is to order the relevant points in a cogent manner. In the early grades it might only be through the spoken word, but later, and especially in the high school, I put the essential bullet points on the board. This is important, because during the presentation on the previous day, especially if it moved in an artistic and organic manner, there will inevitably have been many tangents, which do not necessarily need to be entered into the Main Lesson book. The review allows one to distill the information and compress it into a few pithy points, which can serve as a structure for their individual essays. It brings order and clarity into what was presented the day before, and often sparks new questions as they endeavor to fully understand and digest the material.

During the review one can make them aware of qualitative differences within the material, such as the difference of consciousness between the Middle Ages and the Renaissance. I have noticed that the quality of the essays is far superior if the students write the essays *after* the review. Having discussed the material, heard it summarized, and brought into a cogent form, they are able to arrive at a more solidified personal judgement, and consequently the writing becomes more fluid and clearer. On occasion, when they have had to write an essay on the day of the presentation, due to various circumstances, the results are usually of lower caliber. This certainly happens in high school classes where one has to cover a great deal of material. You pay the price if you rush. They need the night, the time for reflection, and the animated discussions in order for the material to be solidified. Their thinking will have been sharpened, they will have had a stronger feeling connection to the contents, and it will have motivated their will to put down their thoughts on paper with greater confidence. In short: the review can be viewed as a harmonizing process.

Now, having looked back to the previous day's lesson, they are ready to look forward to the new material, which you might have mentioned the day before to whet their appetites and fill them with anticipation of what's to come.

The recall or review can include fruitful discussions, but, as mentioned, one can also introduce the review by reading the previous days writing from the blackboard or from their Main Lesson books, which would then also serve to highlight some language skills, where one could point out interesting words, spellings, or make the students aware of some grammatical point, like the use of active and passive in 6th grade, the tenses in 5th grade, or the parts of speech in 3rd and 4th grade. For the early grades, reading in unison from the board brings the class together. It also gives one the opportunity to see how fluidly individual students can read. From there it is only a small step to combine it with the relevant story material, such as the Norse Mythology, where one could have the students choose appropriate adjectives to describe the various Norse Gods, or verbs that would be most fitting. In this regard, the review also has a vital *skills* component. But in this case, it serves as a stepping stone to the new material. It is not a skills class, however, just like the rhythmical part is not a music or games class. However, it *establishes* the skills, which also means that some practice of the skills takes place. It further illustrates how the Main Lesson contains aspects of the entire day.

Teachers have different approaches, and it is impressive to become witness to their untold innovations. Recently, a young teacher, as she began her review, asked the students to close their eyes and visualize the animal they had covered on the previous day – *without* naming it aloud. Then she asked the students to imagine what the animal was doing, to envision the surroundings, the temperature, how it felt, the sounds. All the while she was encouraging them to picture the scene with the help of as many senses as possible. The students who were in the midst of the Human and Animal block were fully immersed in this "meditation," entering into an imaginary and sensory filled recollection of what they had heard the day before. After letting them bathe in their own pictures that arose, she asked them to think of words that might describe the scene. Then she invited the students to come to the board and write down the words or phrases, quietly. Back in their seats the entire class read all the different words aloud. The communal result was that it gave a rich and stimulating picture of the majestic *lion* in the African savanna. A lively discussion ensued where the students added more points, motivated by what they had inwardly experienced through their recollections, and what they had been exposed to by their classmates. I was especially pleased to note that they pointed out the essential importance of the natural surroundings for the life and well-being of the lion.

Some teachers also ask the students to try and retell the main parts of the presentation, but in reverse. This challenge has an awakening effect, and the students can get quite particular about which events go where, or which scenes are crucial to the story's trajectory. For some the smallest detail might be key, and they will defend and justify their reasons vehemently. Another effective method is to ask them about the characters involved, who they related to most, who played the most vital role, or why a minor character was even included. It is sure to result in unexpected answers and enhance the conversation.

Or you might want to have them focus on certain themes, which means you will direct their attention to the subject matter which you find most important for them to digest, such as major turning points in a story or in a person's biography (in the older grades). You can also have them imagine what might have happened had that experience, meeting, or confrontation *not* happened.

In the lower grades I sometimes had the students act out parts of the story. The fables in 2nd grade lend themselves particularly well to this. In the middle grades the review could also take on the form of a skit, and in the high school, debates are particularly energizing. If two characters of a narrative have different opinions you could stage a conversation between two students where they represent the respective points of view, such as a patrician talking to a plebeian in ancient Roman; or a discussion between an eagle and a buffalo about their lifestyles; or a debate in sixth grade whether Julius Caesar was a tyrant or a hero. This type of debate might go beyond the general boundaries of a review, but it certainly galvanizes their thoughts on the subject after they have learned about Julius Caesar's innovations, the changes to the Roman Empire and to civilization as such.

If the content of the subject matter allows, one can bring in objects or items that relate to that material, such as scale and a feather after telling the Egyptian story of the judgement after death. During the Tragedy and Comedy block in 9th grade I sometimes bring in a small piece of marble that I had picked up from one of the regal seats of the original ancient amphitheater at the foot of the acropolis, just below the Parthenon in Athens (in my foolish youth, before I realized it was not the right thing to do). I then ask them to imagine what that ancient piece of marble might have experienced, who it might have seen and heard, and what it would have learned. I only show it to them *after* presenting the origins of Greek drama and the development of the amphitheater. It has often led to interesting discussions.

For the middle grades one can also divide the class up in two teams and have a quiz review in the form of a jeopardy-style game, which really "tests" their memories in a safe environment. I often played this more at the end of a Main Lesson block, in place of a formal "test." Being in control of the questions, I could make sure that students got asked questions according to their abilities. Again, I did not want to put anybody on the spot. The classes, also in the high school, always enjoy these quizzes. Questions that can be answered with 'true' or 'false' is another variation of the quiz games, or one might get the students to come with the questions themselves, which presupposes that they know the answers. In this case they should write them down first.

During the review one tries to stimulate the students in a variety of ways, helping them to wake up in the head. What they have *grasped* with their hands (physically) and through their feelings (heart), they can now *grasp* with their thinking. There are endless possibilities and the reviews might need as much preparation as the new content of the actual lesson, though care must be taken that it does not take too much time and energy away from the new material.

---

[44] Rudolf Steiner, *Modern Art of Education* (Anthroposophic Press, 2004), August 14, 1923, p. 150.

[45] Rudolf Steiner, *The Kingdom of Childhood* (Anthroposophic Press, 1995) Lecture 4, p. 64.

[46] Rudolf Steiner, *Practical Advice to Teachers* (Anthroposophic Press, 2000), p. 126.

New Material

"We can only be good teachers when we have a living interest in everything happening in the world. Through that interest in the world we must obtain enthusiasm that we need for the school and for our tasks."[47]
~ Rudolf Steiner

IN ALL MY OBSERVATIONS of Main Lessons over the last thirty years it is this section that is most worrisome. The danger is that the presentations of the new material in the elementary school are either too short, underprepared, underdeveloped, or simply merge with the recall. The other extreme is that they swell into a mega lesson or one long drawn-out story, at the end of which the students are either exhausted, pale, or unhealthily flushed. But worst of all is when – as I have witnessed in all too many instances – it does *not* happen at all, the lesson going straight from the review to bookwork. Time spent on new material is around twenty minutes in the lower grades, and approximately 35 to 40 minutes in the middle grades. In high school it is much longer, though it will often take on different forms (see "Main Lesson in the High School").

This is all the more disconcerting as the new content is meant to be the *heart* of the main lesson, the *raison d'être*.

It is what the students anticipate the most, yet what they receive is often not substantial enough. It is a contributing reason why we sometimes lose students in fourth or fifth grade. Not offering any new material is like going without the main meal of the day and getting by on snacks. And like all dinners it needs careful planning. The rhythmical part and the recall are stepping stones leading to this section. They prepare the right mood, helping their souls and minds to become receptive, so that they can absorb what is being presented. The new material constitutes their main academic and soul nourishment of the day, filled with depth of content. It is placed in the morning hour because the minds are most amenable at that time. They have not been tired out yet. We remember that the rest of the day is devoted to skills classes, the arts, and movement. Though the Main Lesson includes the *Hands* and the *Heart*, it is the *Head* that is most emphasized, albeit always artistically, and never in a dry intellectual manner. It is understandable that one cannot always teach an optimal class, but at least, it should be the ideal. Of course, things do interrupt the normal rhythm of the Main Lesson, such as an assembly, a field trip, or a special project like working on a class play, but those are the exceptions. One reason for not presenting new material every day is due to misconceptions about the three-day rhythm. That rhythm runs consecutively, which does not mean that one only brings new material every second or third day (see "Three-day Rhythm").

Often when students say they are not academically challenged, they mean that the lesson was devoid of enough content, genuine substance that engages and meets them in their inner core, quenching their thirst for knowledge, their hunger for the secrets of life revealed, buoyed by moral imagination. And because Waldorf education is an age appropriate education, we differentiate, choose, and prepare our subject matter accordingly. Waldorf teachers are not mere instructors. They strive to be mindful pedagogues, always having bigger perspectives in mind. What do the children need at a certain age, and how does the curriculum support that? Do I have the overview of how a specific historic event fits into the development of human consciousness? To what extent do I take into account the hallmarks of Waldorf education in every lesson, such as going from the whole to the part; relating the material to the human being, whether it's geography, history, chemistry, or mathematics; or the ramifications of age appropriate teaching? In 8th grade, for instance, we study revolutions, because it parallels the revolutionary phase of their lives, when they subtly or overtly rebel against their teachers, parents, and authority as such. We take that into account, show them the consequences of these revolutions, what was achieved, what was sacrificed, destroyed and rebuilt. This defining section of the Main Lesson needs especial care. It requires firm and deliberate protection, similarly to the way the heart is shielded by the rib cage. The whole circulatory system of the body brings the blood to and from the heart. The same is true for this educational enclave. In one way or another, the whole day – including play, chores, after school activities – flows through this focused presentation. This section can be likened to a head of lettuce, where the heart is in the head.

The way it is presented will differ, depending on the subject. Generally speaking, however, it is a time when the students are given the wonderful opportunity to sink into the presentations, where nothing is expected from them, except their rapt attention, which is a form of work. But the teacher needs to earn that attention. We cannot expect the learners to sit quietly and listen if the content is too intellectual, boring or shallow. The ideal lesson is an artistic process, like a musical composition, comprising of exposition, development, and recapitulation, with each of the sections further divided and subdivided. You might start off allegro, and then slow down to lento, followed by an appassionato movement, contrasted with an andante tempo. If you see the class begin to lose focus you can change the rhythm to a wakeful march, or if they are getting too excited, you can balance it out with a melodic minuet. You are drawing them into the material and out of themselves. The sympathy forces are addressed. It's almost as if they are "sleeping" into you. In the *coda* you bring them back from the timeless sphere to the present moment. Part of the return trip is to allow for questions, or some time for discussion. That does not mean that there is no space for questions or discussion during the presentation, should they arise organically. On the contrary, it becomes part of the composition, the musical flow of the class. Their feelings have been stirred and filled, which seeps down, activating their *will* to *do* something, which leads into the next section of the main lesson: bookwork.

The students should get a sense of how important the lesson is to you — existentially so. You are bringing "earth knowledge" to them so that they have the skills and understanding to cope in the world, but always held within the greater universal laws — like the heart interval of the third that is embraced by the prime and the fifth, which gives us the triad — the foundation of much of our Western music. We are readying them for the task ahead in a human centered manner, teaching them capacities, developing skills and faculties. Whatever is presented is heightened and made more effective if it is love imbued, for then they will work for you and appreciate every lesson, no matter what the subject is. Even if they do not "like" grammar they will still do it, because they understand its importance and see your enthusiasm for the lawfulness in the structure of the language. And if one "reads" the students carefully, then one will try different ways of explaining and teaching the material, so that they will at least have a fond relationship to the topic.

A succinct preview of the next day's lesson is worth gold, though it is easy to forget or forego it. It only takes a minute or two, but it sparks their curiosity, and heightens their expectations. But be true to what you promise. Follow through is essential. If promises cannot be kept it builds resentment and diminishes the authority of the class teacher; and the high school students will lose respect for the Main Lesson teacher. This preview can be short and concise, in the form of a few pointed questions, or a statement such as, "Today we covered the life of Michelangelo and were impressed with the painting of the Sistine Chapel and the magnificent sculptures such as the 'David' and 'Pieta.' Tomorrow we will look at an artist who stands in stark contrast to this master. He is also one of the greatest Renaissance artists, but some people claim that his greatest contributions to the world was not through his artistic masterpieces, but something very different." A statement like that will heighten their anticipation. Or, "Today we covered granite, and tomorrow we will examine a versatile rock that has been used in the building of the pyramids and many other constructions, and it owes its existence to the animal world, just as coal came into being through the plant world." Or even simpler: Tomorrow we will look at the remarkable life of Alexander the Great." They are left with the promise of something new the next day. But, in the meantime, they are allowed to "forget" the contents of the lesson until the next day's Main Lesson, when it will be revisited and newly remembered.

---

[47] Rudolf Steiner, *The Foundations of Human Experience* (Anthroposophic Press, 1996) p. 31

Bookwork

"Don't demand anything from the children, but demand it
from yourself and see if the children come along with you"[48]
~ Willi Müller

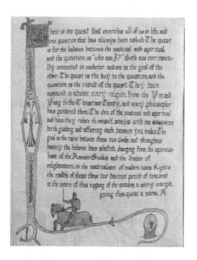

AFTER THE IN-DEPTH presentation of the new material, the children in the elementary school will want to get to work. They have listened as a group, been inspired by the imaginative and thoughtful words of their class teacher, and are now ready for individual work. Bolstered by the mood that's been created they are willing to further digest the given content by embodying it into their Main Lesson books. Some teachers might first give the children a short bathroom and stretch break.

But what actually is the Main Lesson Book? Simply put – it takes the place of the textbook. Instead of receiving books or worksheets on mathematics, geography, history, etc., the students create their own books, based on the presentations of the teacher. In a faculty meeting from May 5th, 1923, Steiner says, "I happily remember how, when I was in school, we did not have any geometry books. [...] A self-written book gives you reason to know what is in it."[49] Steiner goes on to describe how his geometry teacher dictated in a summarized form, the essence of what they had to know. It is one of many places where Steiner criticizes the use of textbooks. For example, in regard to botany and zoology:

> The first thing you have to do is to dispense with all the textbooks. For textbooks as they are written at the present time contain nothing about the plant and animal kingdoms that we can use in teaching. They are good for instructing grown-up people about plants and animals, but you will ruin the individuality of the child if you use them at school.[50]

In regard to physics:

> For physical phenomena also it is just as important to start from life itself. You should not begin your teaching of physics as set forth in the textbooks of today, but simply by lighting a match for instance and letting the children observe how it begins to burn.[51]

And in regard to science as such:

> It is my earnest wish and my duty as leader of the Waldorf school to eliminate from the classroom, whenever possible, everything of a scientific nature that is fixed, including textbooks written in a rigid scientific way.[52]

There are numerous other places where he cautions against using textbooks. Practically speaking, this means that the teacher needs to study the topic in question from many points of view, using an assortment books, so as to get the ideal picture for the children. Many textbooks give a one-sided approach to a subject (we only need to look at how Native Americans have traditionally been portrayed), and it behooves the teacher to study many sources in order to arrive at a broad, yet succinct and balanced summary. That is why it is often said, half-jokingly, that Waldorf teachers do all the work for the students, while the students in a public school do all the work for the teachers.

In creating Main Lesson books, the children learn how to produce beautiful work. Emphasis is put on penmanship, spacing, margins, boarders, diagrams, drawings, and printed and cursive writing. Depending on the grade and subject, rough drafts are written in workbooks before they are corrected and put into final form. It is a process, which includes the ability to process the teachers' lessons, understand the content, and find one's own words to put down on paper. The Main Lesson book is a record of what was presented in the Main Lesson. Each book is unique to the student, and the children take great pride and joy in their work, which many of them treasure for the rest of their lives. The Main Lesson books represent the biography of one's schooling, and give a comprehensive picture of one's overall development.

Careful attention needs to be directed toward the different aspects of this more *will*-dominated section of the Main Lesson. During the transition their books get handed out, according to the tradition and habits of the class teacher. Crayons, pens, and papers get removed from inside the desk. A certain amount of hustle and bustle takes places, which allows them to bridge into the focused bookwork. I always allowed for a modicum of chatter during this transition. It is a form of relaxation and out breathing, before settling down to work. Sometimes, depending on the need, I even had them sing a song, do some jumping jacks or other movement exercise. As mentioned, it's a time they can go to the bathroom if needed, rather than in between when they are supposed to be listening or working. These are the little classroom etiquettes that one can establish from first grade onward, always making sure to modify them according to the students' age and their developing needs. (See "Breathing")

Contingent on the lesson, age group, or grade level, they will quieten down to do a drawing, copy from the board, write their own account, follow a dictation, or, in the case of an arithmetic or geometry block, do math problems or geometric line drawings. Depending on the assignment, the work will be entered directly into the Main Lesson book or into a practice book. After the books, pens, papers, crayons or colored pencils have been taken out and they have settled down to work, one can experience an almost holy mood hovering over the group. In many instances, especially if the presentation fulfilled them, the feeling of well-being is almost palpable. The children are now working on their books with effort and care, according to their own individual abilities.

As a class teacher, I made a point of always working on something directly connected to the classwork together with them, be it a drawing, writing a text on the board, or giving a dictation. I never wanted them to see me idle. On a subconscious level they do not want to see their teacher inactive. They sense it immediately. On one occasion I sat down at my desk to prepare something for another lesson, and immediately one of the girls asked, "What are you doing, Mr. Müller?" as if she knew it had nothing to do with them or the Main Lesson at that moment. On another occasion I simply sat down and looked over the class. Within a minute another student said provocatively, "Not working Mr. Müller?" I had to smile, responding with, "I am just enjoying seeing all of you working so diligently," which seemed to appease her, but I agreed and moments later I got up and did my rounds of helping individual students. We are role models – always in all ways. Or, as Albert Schweizer famously said: *"Example is not the main thing in influencing others – it is the only thing."*

Waldorf teachers are continuously striving to have the children connect as deeply as possible with the respective subjects. The initial presentation, no matter how lively, is still conveyed through thoughts, though the manner of speech and the pictorial approach will already do much to stir the feeling life. However, for the lesson to really take hold of the child, before a true *feeling* for the material can take place, it needs more than the thought content. It relies on all that which precedes and follows the new material.

It must be underscored that the poetry recited in the morning is connected to the new content of the Main Lesson, and that it also enters into the quality of the bookwork. All the different parts of the Main Lesson merge and fructify one another. A final deepening, understanding, and embodying of the content takes place when the thoughts and feelings are brought right down into the written word, the drawings and illustrations. For instance, if the morning presentation dealt with the Voyages of Discovery, they might settle down to do a drawing of a Portuguese caravel, or a full-rigged-ship, knowing that they will be writing about the contents the next day after the review, and into final form on the third day (depending on the rhythm). Thus thinking, feeling, and willing are united, each contributing to the full-bodied experience, ensuring that the whole child is engaged. If the children have been wholly engaged, they will, out of themselves, want to do optimum work, taking great care to make the drawings as beautiful and as exact as possible.

A student who might recall every detail of a history or geography lesson and easily understand formulas and theories, may rush their drawings or not be able to execute a drawing with exactitude. In such cases it is favorable if the teacher attentively guides the child through the drawings. The Main Lesson book, as mentioned, takes the place of the textbooks and therefore needs to be as beautiful as possible, depending on the talents, capacities, and abilities of the students. It is good to develop a healthy pride and reverence for the bookwork. But it needs vigilant and loving guidance. Students can easily get frustrated, and sloppy work should not become a habit.

The same is true for the written work as for the drawings. In the lower grades the text is mostly composed by the teacher, always making sure it is meaningful and as succinct as possible, stating the essence in a condensed manner, with a moral foundation that includes the bigger picture, i.e. within the context of human development throughout the ages, the connection to the world at large, and held within the framework of goodness, beauty and truth. It gets them used to a certain quality, a standard that they, in their own writing, will try to emulate, match, and possibly surpass, which is often the case in high school. Gradually, the students are guided and led toward writing their own essays. However, it should never be forgotten that the original aim of the Main Lesson book is that it takes the place of the textbook. Therefore, the Main Lesson book must contain insightful and pertinent information – something they can refer back to in later years.

If a child has great difficulties in writing their own essays, which is often the case, it should not result in them having a Main Lesson book that says very little of the material covered. Unfortunately, that is what happens in some cases. That is why it is prudent to work in a variety of ways. Giving dictations ensures that the content that you as a teacher are supplying will have depth and the essential information. It tests their own ability to listen, follow, and spell. Even in high school I sometimes give dictations. During a faculty meeting in 1923, Steiner recommended the practice.[53] It is eye opening to see how some of the older students still struggle to keep up or have trouble spelling.

In the lower grades, when I first practiced writing independent essays with the students, it wasn't a given that the essays would make it into their Main Lesson books. Certain criteria had to be met: essential information, cogent writing, and an understanding of the context. Once completed and corrected the students were given the go ahead to copy their work neatly into the Main Lesson book, or they had to write down my version or a version from one of the other students. Sometimes I allowed them to enter the better parts of their own essay.

It is generally frowned upon to copy anything from the board after fifth or sixth grade, but I disagree. There is a great deal that students can learn from copying: use of paragraphs, thesis statement, spelling, syntax, meaning. Copying, if outlined with specific intentions in mind, offers opportunities to develop good writing habits. One can bring consciousness into copying by starting very simply, such as *proofreading* what they have copied, or proofreading each other's work. Or one can ask them to focus on only one specific skill, such as copying something from the board and have them add their own adjectives to all the nouns (or specified nouns), or substituting nouns or noun phrases with a pronoun. There are many other ways of working creatively with copying, such as having them change the tense from the present to the past. It could also include work with paragraphs, punctuation, and spelling. The aim is to build up their writing skills in order to write independently, focusing only on one or two skills at a time.[54] As with everything, one needs to find the right balance and work with the individual capacities in the class. A sense of aesthetics must be developed, which includes a balance between form and content.

That said, one can get the children to write creatively and independently right from first grade. It needs conscious direction, but one can learn a great deal from the students, for they apprehend the world around them in surprising and unfiltered ways. As I was observing a fourth grade recently during the Human and Animal block, the teacher asked the students to describe the different parts of the body. One girl described the head as "*A safe that protects the things inside.*" The concept of the head as a *safe* was unique, true, and poetic.

Once they are ready to get down to work, one should wait till they are all settled before giving the students clear instructions. This is the place for instructions. They want to do good work, and so much depends on the clarity of the teacher. Don't ask them to do anything that is utterly beyond their limits, which might make them feel like failures. Yet, they should be challenged and nudged to surpass themselves. As a rule of thumb, I always let myself be guided by the most able students, while offering as much support as possible for the students who struggle with the work load, offering them modified assignments.

As teachers we all have our quirks – things we find important. For me, it was the headings. I wanted them to respect headings. Headings are key because they tell the reader what the writing is all about, a form of thesis statement. Therefore, to underscore their significance, I wanted them to be written in an artistic manner. Almost daily they heard me say, "Big, bold, and beautiful," when referring to headings. And I always made a point of writing the heading in big bold letters, adding something artistic to highlight the title.

In the high school blocks, most of the bookwork is done outside the Main Lesson, either in a "study hall" or at home. Depending on the subject and the time available, the teacher might allow for bookwork, if it is used efficiently. Putting effort into beautifying the high school Main Lesson books through drawings and illustrations has been criticized by both teachers and some parents. It is argued that too much time is "wasted" on making it "look nice," and that the emphasis should only be on the essays. It has even been argued that students who might want to come to the Waldorf high school are put off because the books look "too beautiful" and they would never be able to produce such high-quality work. What is missed in these arguments is that we are trying to educate the whole person and that it is a matter of having them connect to the material in a variety of ways, which also includes creative writing (in both prose and poetry), sculpture, skits, and, of course, drawings, illustrations, and painting. And in high school we also leave them free to choose how they might want to create their Main Lesson book. One student in tenth grade, for the Odyssey Main Lesson book created a scroll where he wrote the contents in both the Greek script, using Greek letters, and English – all in beautiful calligraphy. It was his own idea. And the writing was top notch. Beautifying the "book" was *not* at the expense of sophisticated and highly cogent writing. It enhanced the work, and allowed him to feel his way into the age of Homer. This particular student got accepted into one of America's Ivy League Universities with a full scholarship.

Some students do indeed struggle more with analytical writing, but excel in art. Through atmospheric drawings of scenes from Wolfram von Eschenbach's *Parzival*, for instance, they are able to enter deeply into the imaginations. That too is a form of knowing – heart intelligence. We all know the expression: *A picture is worth a thousand words.* I am often amazed at what the students were able to capture and convey in their drawings through color, composition, gestures, and other telling details. And who knows what is triggered deep within them? Who are we to judge how deeply the thematic content has touched them? To me it is obvious, when I look at some of the stunning illustrations, that they gained deeper insights into the medieval times than someone who might have written an intellectually sound essay, but without much of an inner connection or immersion. Most of the students take pride and joy in creating unique and aesthetically pleasing work. I never take their work for granted. We live in a world that does not cherish authentic beauty, and it needs to be cultivated, just as the depth of understanding and analytical thinking needs to be cultivated – though I prefer to call it *living thinking.* The practice of aesthetics refines and sharpens the perceptions on a fundamental – almost primal – level, the ripple effects of which enter the stratifications of practical life.

[48] Willi Müller, Long time class teacher and founder of Waldorf Teacher Education, Eugene, Oregon (WTEE).

[49] Rudolf Steiner, *Faculty Meeting with Rudolf Steiner: Volume 2* (Anthroposophic Press, 1998), 12.9.1922, p. 627 The import of Steiner's words in the English translation are insipid compared to how he expressed himself in the original.

[50] Rudolf Steiner, *The Kingdom of Childhood* (Anthroposophic Press, 1995), pp. 36-7

[51] Ibid. p. 111

[52] Rudolf Steiner, *Human Values in Education* (Anthroposophic Press, 2004), pp. 107-108

[53] Rudolf Steiner, *Faculty Meeting with Rudolf Steiner: Volume 2* (Anthroposophic Press, 1998), 12.9.1922, p. 628

[54] Thomas Friedman and James MacKillop, *The Copy Book: Mastering Basic Grammar and Style* (New York: Holt, Reinhart and Winston, 1980).

Story

"Scheherazade is a genius of story medicine. She knows how to tell the right story at the right time. She weaves a story carpet that never ends. She knows when to stop a tale and when to leave it open. She understands the picture language of the soul and speaks it with eloquence. She administers her medicine consciously, carefully. Her tales are not arbitrary; they are carefully chosen to suit the ailing king. By means of her stories she initiates him into his own story."[55] ~ Horst Kornberger

IN THE LOWER SCHOOL the grades teachers often – not always – end the main lesson with a story. This rounding off allows for a moment of silence and settling down before snack recess. The time allotted is brief, between ten and fifteen minutes.

Although I also told stories at the end of the Main Lesson in the first two grades, I found it particularly valuable between the 3rd and 6th grade, but for different reasons. The story content of the respective grades is so vast that it is sheer impossible to do the mythologies justice during the central part of the Main Lesson, especially taking into account the increasing number of subjects one has to teach. There simply is not enough time to cover all the important stories. Although there are scheduled Main Lesson blocks for Hebrew mythology (stories from the Old Testament), Norse mythology, Ancient India, Persia, and so forth, it is nigh impossible to give the students a well-rounded overview of all the dominant sagas and myths. That is where the last portion of the morning lesson comes into play.

While presenting the new material in a humanities' block, such as ancient India or ancient Egypt, one can choose the most thematically important and historically significant tales or mythologies. However, during a math or geometry block one can add some of the remaining stories at the end of class to fill out the picture. During the Egypt block, for instance, one needs to spend a substantial amount of time on the history of Egypt – the dynasties, the geographical aspects, the pyramids, the archeological discoveries, the hieroglyphs, and so forth. However, there are many myths that can be added after the block has ended and one has moved on into another subject. The same is true for Greek history, where there is an even greater choice of mythological stories, which I, for one, was loath to forego, since they shed light on our time and are both relevant and prevalent in modern life, and referred to constantly in literature. In 6th grade the last part of the Main Lesson can be given over to Arthurian legends or the adventures of Parzival.

However, it's not a matter of inundating them with story material. For instance, while telling the story of Osiris during the block on ancient Egypt, one would not need to add another story at the end of the Main Lesson. While teaching subjects like business math or physics, however, it fits well and makes sense. Another option is to use a middle-of-the-day class ("extra-main") for some of these stories, or at the end of the school day, depending on the schedule. It will be contingent on the purpose behind the story and where you want to place it. Stories can be told at the end the Main

Lesson whenever it seems appropriate. I rarely made use of it in 7th and 8th grade, and definitely not in the high school.

Whenever we tell stories, as already mentioned, we must ensure that we speak to the whole child, that they feel the story with their entire body. Thereby we address the child's astral body, out of which something radiates up into the head. In the lower grades it is best to resist the temptation to explain the story, to burden them with abstract concepts, for they will anyway arrive at an understanding of the stories later on. In the first lecture of *Practical Advice to Teachers*, Steiner emphasizes this point: "Try therefore to educate the I-being and astral body from below upward so that the head and heart follow later. Try not to tell the stories in a way that causes the children to reflect and understand them in the head. Tell them in a way that evokes a kind of silent, thrilled awe (within limits) and in a way that evokes pleasure and sorrows that continue to echo after the child has left you, gradually to be transformed into understanding and interest."[56]

---

[55] Horst Kornberger, *The Power of Stories: Nurturing Children's Imagination and Consciousness* (Floris Books, 2008), p. 75.

[56] Rudolf Steiner, *Practical Advice to Teachers* (Anthroposophic Press, 2000), p. 15.

Grace and Snack

Earth who gives to us this food
Sun who makes it ripe and good

Dear Earth, Dear Sun, by you we live
Our loving thanks to you we give[57]

BEFORE SNACK THE Main Lesson is usually brought to a close with a blessing, which cultivates a feeling of gratitude. In this way we continue to foster the fundamental virtue of the first seven-year cycle of life: gratitude. It is the virtue that transforms into the motivating impulse of love. Steiner elucidates on this in *Human Values in Education*: "Love is the virtue that belongs to the second period of life. And after puberty, the experience of love between the change of teeth and puberty become duty, the most inner of human motivation. It becomes the guiding line for life."[58] In the blessing we express our gratitude for what we receive, which transforms into love for what we do, and blossoms into the innermost knowledge of what is demanded of us, our *duty* — fulfilled with *love* and *gratitude*. The blessing draws on the past, strengthens the present, and develops the future.

Everything has been packed away. The children stand and come to inner and outer silence. One can glean a great deal from the tenor of that silence. It is a touchstone moment for the teacher, a moment of taking stock: Was the lesson conducted harmoniously? Did I bring enough content? Was I able to resolve an underlying social issue? Did I meet their needs? Are they fulfilled? Did I achieve the hallmarks of the Waldorf ideals? That is, did I connect the subject matter to the human being, go from the whole to the part, teach imaginatively, conduct the class in a rhythmical and musical manner? Did I make them laugh and "cry" at least once during the lesson? Did I lead the children through the entire zodiac of the senses during this Main Lesson? Of course, these questions remain just below the surface of the teacher's consciousness, but are nevertheless experienced palpably as a mood.

In those settling seconds before we say or sing grace, the teacher can see in their faces whether they are content, enlivened, or upset. All the senses become like ears, listening to the well-being of the class and each student. The teacher can feel that sense of life within herself. Often one feels touched by grace.

Many schools have a designated timeframe for eating for the lower grades, usually about ten minutes. This ensures that all children eat something and don't get tempted to rush outside to play without having eaten anything. It is prudent to bring up the issue of food in parent evenings. The ideal is to have the students eat healthy food and to come up with guidelines in regard to sharing food in the class. If the parents can arrive at an agreement with the teacher regarding the types of food allowed in the classroom, it makes it easier for all people involved, especially because some students have dietary restrictions and needs.

Depending on the grade or the day, some teachers like to read to the class while they eat. It has a different mood to telling a story. It gives the teacher a chance to read a great book to the students while they eat their food in a quiet and measured manner. It is also a fine opportunity for them to hear, thus emulate, oral reading proficiency. After that the children can go out to enjoy recess. Play is a form of digestion. The main lesson has ended.

---

[57] A much-loved grace spoken in the lower school.

[58] Rudolf Steiner, *Human Values in Education: The Foundations in Waldorf Education* (Anthroposophic Press, 2004), Lecture 6.

PART TWO

PART TWO

Breathing

"Of all the relationships humans have to the physical world, the most important is breathing."[59] ~ Rudolf Steiner

THE HUMAN BEING is a rhythmical being through and through. We are enveloped by multi-rhythms, act according to these rhythms, and feel out of sorts when thrown out of rhythm. We wish to ride the flow of rhythm, to get in sync with rhythm, and sometimes we aim to change our rhythms, to reestablish new rhythms, or to become more aware of the power of life's diverse rhythms. *Breath* is softened rhythm, cushioned rhythm, rounded rhythm. It surrounds the pulse as the lungs surround the heart like protective wings. The pulse orders the breath from within. The breath balances the breath from without. Breath and pulse are intimately connected, the one affecting the other, closely sensing and listening to each other, allowing us to live. The human being is a musical being through and through. Steiner states:

> All rhythmic experience bases itself on the mysterious relationship between breathing and the heartbeat, the circulation of the blood. One thus can say that while the melody is carried from the heart to the head on the stream of breath — and therefore

in an outer slackening and inner creation of quality
– the rhythm is carried on the waves of the blood
circulation from the heart to the limbs, and in the
limbs it is arrested as willing. From this you can see
how the musical element really pervades the whole
human being[60].

For a teacher it is helpful to meditate periodically on the
significance of the breath as it relates to the pulse, just as we
meditate on the straight and curved line before entering first
grade, and many times thereafter. When we are born, we
take in our first breath, and when we die, we release our last
breath. We begin our earthly life with an inhalation and end
it on an exhalation. We inspire and expire a little with every
breath, we live and die with every breath. Something enters
and something leaves. We take in the new and give off the
old. Tension is created, and tension is released. Every breath
transforms the air. Light and darkness resides in every
breath. With each breath the polarity is equaled out – a yin
yang experience. We expand and we contract. Sometimes
faster, sometimes slower, depending on the circumstances.
No breath is ever repeated. Each breath is unique, imbibing
and gifting soul experiences. Little births and deaths every
time we breathe – 18 times in just one minute. How
wonderful!

And it is all based on the lawful relationship between the
breath and the pulse: four pulses to one breath (in and out).
Meditating on this relationship and its universal magnificence
can be overpowering, can boggle the mind – or fill one with
humble wonder at the illimitable wisdom of the world.
Understanding the meaning of just one breath allows us to
comprehend the connection between the human being and
the vast expanse of the cosmos. *To see the World in one small
breath*. Within the confines of one breath we can perceive the
unity between the divine and the temporal. Heaven and
earth are one. And Steiner, when he elaborates on these
connections is able to clarify this relationship in such a way

that it throws light onto diverse aspects of our existence, including education.

The ratio is 1:4, which can also relate to the approximate ratio of nitrogen and oxygen in the air (20% of oxygen to 80% nitrogen, or to be specific, 21% to 78%). The rhythm of the pulse and breath is foundational to all music and poetry. In one minute, we have 18 breaths to 72 pulses, and we breathe 25,920 times a day on average. What makes this number so awe inspiring is that it correlates to the Platonic year. This period of time for one complete cycle of the equinoxes around the ecliptic is 25,920 years, which corresponds to the number of breaths we take, on average, every day. In other words, that is how long it takes for the sun to move through the zodiac. This is also called the Great Year (modern day astronomy usually vacillates between 25,772 and 26,000 years, which is close to 25,920). We can read about this cycle not only in Plato's work, but also in the world's most ancient text, the Vedas, where the so-called Yuga Cycles are written about and explained. The correspondence between the number of breaths we take in a day and the great Platonic Year is astounding, whether we accept the reality of the spiritual world or not. It shows how we, as humans, are a microcosm of the macrocosm, how the small fits into the large. We are intimately connected to the Great Platonic Year with our breath and our pulse. The macrocosm lives within us.[61]

~

When I first began teaching at Hawthorne Valley Waldorf School in upstate New York, Rudolf Copple was already in his mid to late eighties. He had been a Waldorf teacher in New York City, and before that a eurythmist. As a distinguished elder he often mentored teachers and observed their classes when he first moved up to Hawthorne Valley. Patrice Maynard, who was privileged to have had him sit into one of her classes, often talked about Rudolf Copple and his comments, accompanied by smiles and nods of agreement. His main point was that the Main Lesson, with its distinct sections, needs to *breathe*. It is exactly this 'breathing' process between the different segments of the Main Lesson that he found lacking in almost all of the classes he visited, adding that it was especially noticeable in America. The more I began to mentor, observe, and evaluate teachers, the more I also noticed this quality. Some classes felt tight and breathless, others needed literal and figurative oxygenation, and frequently the sections merged into one another so that the 'breathing' felt shallow. There were even times when I was not sure what block was being taught.

When to breathe *in* and when to breathe *out* – that is the question. Education has a great responsibility to guide correct breathing. Knowing the importance of breathing is a good starting point. We incarnate with each inhalation, and we "excarnate" with each exhalation – ever so gently. As teachers we not only have to observe and sensitively listen to the quality of the class, but read the students in front of us. In previous sections of this book we have already seen how some parts of the lesson are geared towards the one or the other: expansion or contraction. But, in order to achieve healthy breathing in the classroom we have to practice working with the different segments of the lesson, especially within the long morning lesson. The harmonious duration of each section creates balanced breathing. Teachers become composers and conductors and each Main Lesson is a musical composition conducted by us.

Transitions: Each transition, no matter how small, contributes to the healthy flow of the lesson. A smooth transition can be achieved with a song, poem, clapping, rhythmical walking, or a combination of the above. Sometimes a mere moment of silence will suffice. Depending on what we choose – and there are many variations – it will have a calming or enlivening effect. This ongoing contraction and expansion will serve the needs of the class. We are 'breathing' from one section into another. It lets the students know that we are leaving something behind and entering a new phase of the lesson. And each segment of the lesson will call forth a variation in the breathing. Within each lesson the students' breathing needs to be increased and slowed down, in conjunction with the heart rate. The rhythms of the heart affect the respiratory system. I recall observing a second grade where the teacher had the children walk the balance beam on their way to collecting the Main Lesson book in the transition between the new material and bookwork. It was wonderful to observe the students, one after the other make their way across the beam. It did not take long, but during those few moments they activated their senses of movement and balance, which, in turn, subtly connected them to the cognitive senses: those of the word and hearing, respectively. A perfect transition.

Content: While we are in front of the students, we are delivering content, whether it is giving instructions, wiping the board, or teaching the new material. Content too, is part of the yin and yang of the lessons – the contraction and the expansion. If we have covered serious content such as the biography of Nero – the bad-gone-mad Roman emperor – we can balance it out by contrasting his heinous rulership with the achievements of emperor Trajan, known as *optimus princepts*, the "best ruler." If we pull them in too far (contraction), then we need to release the tension (expansion) through a humorous anecdote or a joke. Steiner explicitly remarked that in every successful Main Lesson the children should laugh and cry at least once. Gravity and levity within the soul and body needs to be part and parcel of our daily lessons. The children's actual breathing is either sped up or slowed down with everything we do in the classroom, with the songs we sing, the poetry we recite, the games we play, or the moments of stillness and the quiet listening. There are times when the children are sitting at the edge of their chairs holding their breaths at an exciting part of the story, or they exhale with relief when the tension has resolved itself, leaning back in their chairs.

However, there are also long-term consequences that are directly connected to *how* we deliver the content, which effects the breathing of the children far into the future. Waldorf education is all about artistic, lively, enthusiastic teaching that addresses the whole child. Yet, the greatest challenge in our time is not to succumb to abstractions and intellectuality. Rudolf Steiner, during his last public lectures in 1924, Stuttgart said,

> If we overstrain the intellect and are not able to pass over into the pictorial, the breathing process in the child gets into disorder in a delicate, subtle way. The child becomes congested, as it were, in a weakness of the out-breathing process. [...] [And] the child falls victim to a kind of subconscious nightmare, if education is too intellectualistic between the seventh and fourteenth years. A kind of inner, intimate nightmare comes into being that remains with the organism, and leads in later life to asthmatic conditions or other diseases connected with a turgid breathing process.[62]

Another element of healthy classroom breathing is the length of each segment. If, for instance, we tell a story for too long, then they will get flushed in an unhealthy manner, even if they are enjoying the story; and if we do not offer enough new material, or only tell a small slice of the story, they will feel shortchanged.

Successful breathing in a classroom is when the students know they are being carried by the rhythm of the lesson. With orchestrated transitions and insightful use of the content and physical activity the two hours will fly by, and the students will go into recess feeling fulfilled. The threefold nature of the human being – head, heart, and hand – will have been addressed. In short: correct breathing is finding the balance between form and freedom. Nor should we forget that the way we conduct the morning lesson will also affect the subsequent classes.

A further aspect of *breathing* relates to how we plan our various Main Lessons (see "Preparing for the Main Lesson"). After a block has ended, we let the subject matter go to sleep, to be reawakened again either later on in the year or in the following year. Steiner underscores the importance of forgetting and remembering on many different occasions. The gestation period allows the material to mature and transform. Learning is never linear. It grows like a plant, where for a while nothing seems to happen and then nodes on the stem appear and new leaves sprout or flower. The plant is an apt metaphor for learning and growth. The *resting* or *forgetting* period in between lets concepts take root, flourish, and bear fruit. When one comes back to the material, the students re-experience the contents in a new and living manner, and can forge ahead with renewed interest and incentive. It puts things into context and deepens the experience. A new relationship to the subject is cultivated and often the students find fresh inroads to the content. I have also observed that if there was an antipathy toward something, for one reason or other, it often falls away, has transformed itself, or is simply no longer an issue. Understanding something is a mysterious thing. In one's own life one can observe how frequently problems reveal or resolve themselves, possibly only after many years – even decades. But the seed needs to be planted.

The tremendous importance of breathing and how it is intimately connected to the three-part system of the human body is mentioned in the very first lecture of *The Foundations of Human Experience*, where Steiner states "that children cannot yet of themselves breathe properly, and that education consists in teaching proper breathing."[63] This middle realm of breathing is intimately connected on the one hand to the metabolism, especially in regard to the blood circulation, and on the other hand with the nerve-sense life, where the cerebral-spinal fluid is pressed into the brain with each in-breath, and back into the body with each out-breath. Steiner then goes on and brings it into connection with the child's inability "to create harmony between two parts of the human being, between the temporal body and the spiritual-soul." Nor can the child "complete the transition between sleeping and waking in a way appropriate to human beings. [...] [They] cannot take everything they have experienced physically into the spiritual world, process it there and then bring the results of this work back to the physical plane."[64] And this is where the teacher plays a significant role. Whatever we bring to them in the classroom and at school in regard to proper breathing will support proper rhythm between waking and sleeping.

> As teachers, we cannot give children anything from the higher worlds. What human beings receive from the higher worlds comes to them during sleep. All we can do is use the time children spend in the physical plane to help them gradually to become able to take what we do with them into the spiritual world. Then, what they carry in can flow back into the physical world as strength, strength they can bring from the spiritual world to become real human beings in physical existence.[65]

So, what else can we do to help them in this respect? Steiner, in the same lecture, mentions that the greatest effect on the students is through *who we are* and the spiritual striving we have undertaken throughout our lives. This, in turn, will influence the content of our lessons, down to the smallest detail. Part of what we have to teach in our time is very abstract, but if we imbue the material with enthusiasm, life, and inner reverence, we are also teaching them the right relationship with their sleep life. They then take into sleep the moral underpinnings and ideals we have instilled within them. Whatever has moved them inwardly, motivated them in their life of virtues, prodded their conscience, will be transformed through the ongoing rhythm of waking and sleeping. These resultant moral strengths, will be experienced as feelings of well-being toward all that is good, true and beautiful. Each lesson is a seed, which fosters and strengthens the initial divide between the spiritual and physical, gradually bringing the spirit-soul and the corporeal into harmony. When the children bring their soul experiences, their sympathetic understanding and connection to all that is noble and good into their life of sleep, then these attributes can be deepened and intensified through the hierarchical beings. The reinforced astral body then reenters the etheric and physical body, subtly changing the rhythm of the breath. These settled soul forces thus modify the breathing so that it becomes ever more balanced. The connections to the moral nourishment of the lessons lives on in a refined way within the rhythms of the breath and can, over time, become a general mood of soul. Gradually it becomes an inner orientation toward the moral realm.[66]

Knowledge takes time. Understanding takes time. Acquiring skills takes time. Do we as teachers label students too early? Are they defined by those labels? Especially in our present age, the students want to be seen for who they are, and not be reduced to a label such as ADD, ADHD, relegated to a place on the spectrum, or called Indigo children, Star children, or whatever, even though legitimate assessments have a definite place in our understanding of these students and how we can help and support them.

I have observed many students make tremendous strides over the years, some of them nearly miraculous. I recall a student in high school who had the hardest time reading and writing, though he was bright, attentive and highly insightful. Fully supported by his parents and teachers, his school requirements were drastically modified, and it said as much in the reports. Five or six years after he graduated, I suddenly received a card from him (I had been his advisor) inviting me to his graduation. After a few years as a woodworker he had enrolled in college and become an architect. I was deeply moved. Students have different learning styles, so we have to trust them while giving them the support they need. Similarly, we had a student who barely wrote any of the assigned essays until his senior class, no matter how much he was encouraged and prodded. We allowed him to help out on the farm after Main Lesson (a suggestion that came from him). When senior year came, he suddenly took off, producing complete Main Lesson books in all of the blocks. Certainly, in my *Faust* block his Main Lesson book was one of the most comprehensive and insightful books of the entire class: a truly stunning achievement. There was evidence of his development in earlier years by his strikingly perceptive and insightful comments during the class discussions, but he hadn't yet had the capacity to put them down on paper. He far surpassed our expectations.

This is important to bear in mind, because of the growing trend in an increasing number of Waldorf schools to push the academics right from first grade, claiming the children won't know how to read and write if not more time is invested in a whole array of cleverly thought out curricula, even recommending that the school day be lengthened. One forgets that the students who are inwardly not ready, will simply not "get" some concepts, no matter how much we try to "stuff" it into them. In this regard it behooves us to recall the famous quote by W.B. Yeats, "Education is not the filling of a pail, but the lighting of a fire." Rudolf Grosse, longtime teacher at the Rudolf Steiner-Schule in Basel, Switzerland, writes in his insightful and wide-ranging book, *Erlebte Pädagogik* (Experienced Pedagogy), "There are students who reject any intellectual learning and are unable to achieve or perform anything that is brought to them in an abstract form before they have reached adolescence. It infiltrates them as little as water seeping through the skin. They might be considered dullards, whereas their souls are still at home in the very different realms of the pictorial and imaginal consciousness. Once they have bridged puberty, then one can barely recognize them in their transformed being, and in the shortest time they have easily caught up with all that which was impossible to teach them beforehand."[67] Rudolf Grosse goes on to give a few remarkable examples of students who had undergone such noteworthy transformations. In the same paragraph Grosse quotes Steiner in reference to a "slow" student: "You'll see, he will open his head when he reaches 9th grade."[68] The task of the teacher, however, is to distinguish between those students who have legitimate learning disabilities that do indeed need to be addressed therapeutically, and those who simply need more time. It is important, in these cases, to work closely together with the parents and, if possible, the school doctor and the remedial teacher.

We can therefore come to a greater understanding that there are different rhythms involved in the development of breathing. The pedagogical respiratory system demands to be observed ever more closely by teachers and understood in terms of an expanded picture of the human being.

---

[59] Rudolf Steiner, *The Foundations of Human Experience* (Anthroposophic Press, 1996) p. 40

[60] Rudolf Steiner, *The Inner Nature of Music and the Experience of Tone* (Spring Valley, New York: The Anthroposophic Press, 1983), p. 67-68.

[61] Wilhelm Hoerner, *Kosmische Rhythmen im Menschenleben* (Stuttgart: Urachhaus, 1990)

[62] Rudolf Steiner, *The Essentials of Education* (London: Rudolf Steiner Press, 1968), p.24.

[63] Rudolf Steiner, *The Foundations of Human Experience* (Anthroposophic Press, 1996), p. 41.

[64] Ibid. p. 41-42.

[65] Ibid. p. 42.

[66] Ernst Michael Kranich, „Die Verbindung des werdenden Menschen mit den Kräften des Moralischen." Kranich, (Hrsg.), *Moralische Erziehung: Beiträge zur Pädagogik Rudolf Steiners* (Stuttgart: Verlag Freies Geistesleben, 1994) p. 37.

[67] Rudolf Grosse, *Erlebte Pädagogik: Schicksal und Geistesweg* (Dornach: Verlag am Goetheanum, 1998), p. 96 (loosely translated by the author).

[68] Ibid.

Three-Day Rhythm

"By forcing the intellectual powers of children, we hinder their growth; we liberate those forces, however, by approaching the intellect through art. [...] Teaching thus begins with imagery, not intellect. The teacher-child relationship is pervaded by music and rhythm, and thus we attain the necessary degree of intellectual development in children."[69] ~ Rudolf Steiner

SO MUCH IN WALDORF education has to do with rhythm. The more we weave the various rhythms together, the more harmonious our lessons will be, which strengthens the habit body of the child and infuses the learner with life forces. We have to take rhythm seriously. The three-day rhythm is another example of consciously working with the curriculum in order to reap optimal results. Its implementation aids the whole child, in that it supports and strengthens the memory, supplies a solid foundation for the development of the intellect, and brings the content right down into the will through movement and other artistic pursuits.

There is some confusion about the three-day rhythm. Simply put (though not pedantically): on day one we introduce the new material; on day two we review, solidify, and develop it; and on day three we finalize and bring it to conclusion. The misconception easily arises that new material only gets brought every three days. But no: new material is introduced every day, though it follows the three-day sequence.

The significant element is the time span in between the classes because it allows the subject matter to settle and be assimilated. The emphasis is on the first two days, which is why it is also considered to be more of a two-day rhythm. However, conclusions are important; they sum up and contain the essence of the pedagogical content and, if we add one more day to the process, we are supporting the maturation process. In reality, the situation oftentimes demands that the conclusion is brought at the end of the second day, though the written work often needs another day to reach its final form. What is important is to arrive at a conclusion, which brings closure to the topic until it is brought up again in the future.

The three-day rhythm is closely aligned with the concept of *breathing* (see "Breathing"). As is mentioned in various places, it takes into account the sleep life. On the first day we introduce the *new material.* The students listen and absorb the contents. We generally do not ask them to do any written work on the presented material on the same day, no matter which grade. However, they might be asked to do an artistic activity that corresponds to the new material, such as drawing a dandelion, or they might work on a cover page if it also happens to be the first day of the block.

On day two the new material of day one is *reviewed* (see "Review"). During this review, the children remember and relive the previous day's lesson, discuss it, express their understanding of the material, offer opinions, judgements or conclusions. The children, having integrated the new material during the night, will have a more personal and clearer relationship to it. The teacher might lead the students through various activities which will reinforce what has been learned or offer other perspectives. Now they are ready to write on the material reviewed, which will take on different forms depending on the grade level and current Main Lesson block.

On the third day, the conclusion will take the form of a quick overview and summary of the essential elements of the content, which might include putting the writing into final form or reading aloud the written text on the board one last time (in the lower grades), after which the topic is left behind, until one returns to it at a later date. Conclusions or definitions must be avoided at the beginning of the cycle.

To restate: Day 1), *introduction.* Day 2), *review* and development. Day 3), *conclusion,* letting go. However, what is not so easily recognized and practiced is that the three-day rhythm does not repeat itself every three days, but that the *rhythms run concurrently to one another*. It is a form of parallel motion, or a three-tiered cycle. It bears repeating, but I have talked to many teachers who are under the impression that they only have to introduce new material every second or third day. Part of the misunderstanding lies in the fact that the teachers often only assign the written work on the third day, the day of the conclusion. Some teachers have a two-day cycle for new material and a three-day cycle for the written work. It is easy to recognize that implementing and upholding such a rhythm will be difficult. However, this is one of the major reasons why we do not get enough content covered in our Main Lessons, why we end up rushing through our curriculum at the end of the block, and why not enough comprehensive work gets done in class. It is imperative that this three-day rhythm is clearly understood. Bottom line: every day the students should receive new material, unless there are legitimate extenuating circumstances. Children will not complain about being under challenged if they receive new material every day.

To reaffirm one more time for good measure in different words: On the first day of the block we are getting started with the rhythm. There is nothing yet to review or conclude. But we introduce the new material. After that the children usually do a drawing that encapsulates the block. For example, they might draw a picture of a Greek temple on the front cover or the first page of the book on Ancient Greece, and add a short poem or verse that will be recited in the morning for part of the block and serve as a key theme.

However, on day two you will review what was brought on day one, followed by the new material. Hence, day two includes a new beginning of the three-day rhythm. But, still no conclusion. For the bookwork they will write on day one's theme (either in their practice books or copying a text into their main lesson books), and also finish their drawing, or start on a new drawing or illustration.

On the third day of the block, a small portion of the review will be devoted to the conclusion of what was introduced on day one. A brief summing up is all that is needed, which might include a reading of the text that has been written. But on day three you will continue to review the new material of the previous day, after which, once again, the new material of the day will be introduced. After the first initial three days, you now have all three elements. *This established cycle now continues throughout the rest of the block.* Francis Edmunds describes the process in the following way:

> The process of learning is an assimilative one and follows a definite course. What is absorbed through observation and thought by day sinks into deeper strata of the soul at night and returns next day to the consciousness again, confirmed in feeling and in will. This is a three-day process. What is taught on one day is recalled in conversation on the second day and gathered together, written down and given its final form on the third day. What is merely apprehended on the first day returns enriched by personal feeling on the second day and becomes part of oneself by the third day.[70]

In the grades I tended to divide the blackboard into three sections, one for each day. On the third day I would generally erase everything that had been covered on the first day, unless some students were not quite finished with a drawing or a piece of writing. Exceptions may include detailed drawings such as a map during a geography block or a drawing of Yggdrasil, the mythic tree from Norse mythology, which might remain throughout the block. In such cases it allowed me to add names or labels over the course of the lessons.

Of course, in practice, it does not always run so smoothly, and the focus is more on the two-day rhythm. You might not be able to implement all three aspects for any number of reasons. In reality, it toggles between a two- and three-day rhythm. The bookwork does tend to have a bit of a different rhythm and it cannot always keep up with the review and new material. In that regard things shift somewhat. Furthermore, there are children in the class who have different temperaments and are on different academic levels. Some children, especially the perfectionists, will want to spend much longer on a drawing, whereas some are done within minutes. The same is true with the writing. Or there is an imbalance between the three sections. This all impedes the flow of the three-day-rhythm. And that is fine. It's what we aim for that is important. There is ample room for creative spontaneity and improvisation; as long as we don't give up and just let things roll along haphazardly.

On looking more closely at the three aspects of the 3-day-rhythm the teacher might notice that she spends too much time on the review, or alternatively too little time on the new material. To recapitulate: *every day* we endeavor to *conclude* (day 3), *review* (day 2), and add *new material* (day 1). If this three-tiered rhythmic cycle can become second nature to us, then we can achieve a great deal in the classroom. The effectiveness of this approach is embedded in the night and sleep life, which plays such a significant and central role in Waldorf education.

[69] Rudolf Steiner, *A Modern Art of Education* (Anthroposophic Press, 2004), August 11, 1923, p. 109.

[70] Francis Edmunds, *An Introduction to Steiner Education: The Waldorf School* (Forest Row: Sophia Books, 2004), p. 93.

Main Lesson in the High School

"Essentially, there is no education other than self-education. We have to provide the conditions where children can educate themselves according to their own destinies."[71] ~ Rudolf Steiner

AFTER GRADUATING MY eighth grade we moved from Eugene, Oregon to the Hawthorne Valley Waldorf School in Harlemville, upstate New York, where I became a high school humanities teacher, which included, apart from the Main Lessons and middle of the day classes, the 10th and 12th grade play productions, chorus, as well as any number of rotating electives. The greatest wakeup call I experienced in my transition from the lower school to high school was the rhythm of the Main Lessons. Middle grade habits had no place in the high school. The fundamental differences included exceptionally brief opening activities, markedly longer presentations, and curtailed bookwork, necessitating more homework.

Though I had adjusted fairly well to the changing needs of the children from first grade through to eighth, I now had to make some quick, abrupt, and conscious amendments. First off, noticing that the rhythmical part was vastly reduced (and with some teachers, almost nonexistent, except for possibly a short poem to set the tone for the block) I had to come up with alternatives. Though I shortened my 'tuning up' time, I still recited poetry, did occasional speech exercises, and sang songs to highlight the thematic content – or sang for the sheer joy of singing.

The manner in which the opening activities are conducted in the high school does depend partly on the teacher, but more on the respective block. In the History through Music class in 11th grade, the singing of songs takes precedence, apart from reciting a poem or two connected to music. The music block also allows for a greater spectrum of activities, which can include a drumming circle, musical improvisations (with and without instruments), and even dancing. These expanded activities do not, of course, happen every day. On most mornings it will still only be a couple of songs and a poem before moving right along into the heart of the lesson. However, I often rearrange my musical activities so that they do not only happen in the beginning, but are dispersed throughout the rest of the Main Lesson, in conjunction with the respective curriculum. For example, if we are talking about medieval music, we might sing a Gregorian chant at that moment, making it part of the lesson.

The 9th grade Tragedy and Comedy block also presents opportunities for a slightly extended rhythmical part. Drama exercises, skits, and an array of improvs suitably support the plays one reads and the study of drama's development through the ages. In many instances I incorporate the drama work after the recall and the new material, which breaks up the main lesson homogeneously. The polar aspects of tragedy and comedy serve as an appropriate transition between the middle grades and high school. During the activities, I can observe how the students move, react, listen, speak, project, and work within a group. And we laugh a lot. In that sense the drama exercises are a sophisticated and apropos expression of "circle time."

In all the high school Main Lessons I have also found it helpful to start the morning with a short writing exercise, such as a group poem, prompt, or a leading question. This gets them moving in their minds, as opposed to physical movement in the early grades. The effect is similar in its balancing and harmonizing effect. The act of thinking by themselves or quietly within a group writing exercise helps them to incarnate and to wake up.

The other big difference, as stated, is the length of time at one's disposal for the new material – of which there is a great deal more than in the grades. The students have stronger mental stamina and can stay with themes for a longer period of time. However, this too took time to master. One cannot simply lecture to them, which can easily get boring, especially if it is presented intellectually, something one has to continuously safeguard against. It gives rise to the question: how does one bring healthy breathing into the high school Main Lesson? Some aspects, of course, remain the same, such as depth of content, enthusiasm, and bringing the subject matter alive through the imagination. However, the adolescent's yearning and inner quest for *ideals* must be met, with a slightly different emphasis in each grade. Furthermore, they expect the teacher to be utterly authentic and expert in their field. Of course, honest teachers will never fully feel like experts, but at least they must have an educated passion for the discipline they are teaching. This inner state of the teacher is felt by the students and they respond to it (though, alas, one does not always reach everybody).

Most of the breathing – expansion and contraction – that takes place in the high school must be incorporated within the delivery and the breakdown of the time at one's disposal, since the lesson is no longer comfortably cushioned by the framework of the rhythmical part and the bookwork. One has to make sure that there is a balance between listening to new content, getting into discussions, and activities related to the material. If only a handful of students participate in the discussions, others might tune out. The high school teacher is also more prone to lifeless presentations and the deadening influences of abstractions, and it must be underscored that the use of imagination and an artistic approach is just as important in the high school as in the early grades.

Most presentations are frontal, due to the general nature of imparting knowledge, but one can break it up in various ways such as sitting in a circle, where one can discuss or read excerpts in a more intimate setting, or break out into groups. However, having them work on a group project or discuss certain thematic content, needs careful planning and preparation, to avoid the groups becoming a "free for all" where they succumb to laughter and chatter about whatever. Oral presentations by the students make for a welcome and constructive change. It fosters public speaking, takes them out of their comfort zone, and gives them the chance to be actively involved, while offering them the experience of what it is like to stand in front of the class and lead a lesson. For most Waldorf students it comes easily, because they have had ample opportunity in the lower grades to present something in front of people. Nevertheless, it helps to clearly delineate the requirements and expectations so as to avoid an abundance of hemming and hawing or three-sentence presentations. Occasionally, there are students who feel traumatized by the very idea of having to speak alone in front of people, even their own class. If all coaxing and gentle persuasions fails, I allow them to write out what they would have said. Not to make allowances will result in them possibly not showing up on the day of their allotted time to present.

The review also plays an important role in the high school. Because the students receive so much new material every day, there is even more of a need for them to digest and 'forget' the material for a night. It gives the teacher the time to fully enter into the lesson, see where it takes the class, and where the class takes the material. During the presentation of the new material I fill the blackboard with all sorts of notes, drawings, and diagrams to underscore the thematic content and essential facts and pertinent information. The lesson takes on a life of its own. Though thoroughly prepared I make allowances for the lesson to take us to all sorts of unexpected places. My blackboard becomes increasingly messy and ends up looking somewhat like a Jackson Pollock painting. But it only appears convoluted, for the points hang together though spread apart. And that's when the review on the following day becomes essential. On a purely practical level I can pull all the sundry threads together, collect the disparate pieces and write them cogently on the board, based partly on what comes from the students and what the material demands. Their essays often directly reflect the contributions during the review. And, as was pointed out earlier, one has the opportunity to add and fill in the missing pieces and forgotten bits of information. A great deal often comes in the way of questions. In fact, sometimes the best discussions occur during the review rather than during the new presentations – for which I always allow ample time.

High School students are looking for broader perspectives, deeper insights, and soul-spiritual riches that throw light on what it means to be a human being. They are still finding out how to function in society. They are searching for answers to the riddles of life and themselves. This must be offered to them in a free and unencumbered manner through the subject matter, be it the humanities or the sciences. In literature classes where one tackles meaningful, universal thoughts, it is essential that the teacher can guide them through the thematic maze and supply the missing content that can shed light on the mysteries of the world and life on earth. If the students are met with ideas that can transform into ideals, which can continue to grow and change throughout their lives, then we are truly teaching for life. Even the smallest remark can have the deepest, most far reaching effects and consequences. A lot of what we teach is a bit like a time bomb – the "aha" moment might come almost at once, within minutes, or only after many years. While the teacher is in front of the students everything counts. As educators we are in the job of furthering relationships, of instilling the ability to think logically. Living thinking leads to free thinking and clear assessments of the world and themselves.

Whenever – at the end of the Main Lesson – the students say, "What, is it already over – wow, that went fast," then I know that something worked. Of course, that does not always happen, but it is satisfying when it does. However, it is just as important NOT to only display one's own learning, to simply hold forth – no matter how grand it might be, how much you think they might gain from it, or how well structured the lesson is. More important is what we can coax and draw out of them. Our in-depth knowledge should equip us with the tools for asking the right questions that get them excited to enter into a voyage of discovery, to examine and explore the subject matter themselves – then they will own the material so much more than if we told them everything. There will always be enough for you, the teacher, to say. But to give them the space to find their voices, that too is an art that needs cultivating (and which leads to right breathing). Besides, the students have a great deal to contribute and there is no denying that many surpass us in a whole range of ways – if we truly listen to them and appeal to their essential beings.

Apart from this greater emphasis on the new material and content, there is much less time devoted to in-class bookwork, though there are a few exceptions, such as in the projective geometry block. That said, the normal time set aside in lower school for the students to work on their Main Lesson books is no longer available. In most cases the lessons, group work, discussions and sundry activities last right up to the end of class.

In-class bookwork should only be assigned if all the students actually get down to work, without becoming distracted, claiming they can work better at home, or end up completing work due for another class. The high school teacher no longer has the same kind of "authority" as the class teacher, and "forcing" them to work in class is to be avoided. If only some students get down to serious work it becomes a waste of time for the rest of the class and goes against economical teaching.

On the other hand, loading them up with too much homework, just because they are unable to complete the work in school, will result in potentially shoddy work. It calls for sensitivity. Does the homework make sense? Is it too much? Will they benefit from the work? Does it offer a learning experience? Can it potentially arouse enthusiasm? Will they enjoy immersing themselves in the work? I am continuously trying to find the balance, often failing. It also means putting oneself into their shoes and their busy schedules.

On average a high school student has school until three in the afternoon. Many students are enrolled in sports, but also in sundry extracurricular activities such as painting, photography, drama club, etc. or private music, ballet, or dance classes. On top of that most students have jobs at least once a week. And that is not including their daily commute, which can, in the case of some students, take over an hour, one way. When do they have time to rest, to chill, to eat? When the sports teams have away games, the time crunch is further exacerbated. I saw the toll it took on my three sons, when they would arrive back from a basketball game at 10 p.m. and were still confronted with a backpack full of homework. As Main Lesson teachers we should bear this in mind when assigning homework. Furthermore, we have to remember that the special subject teachers also demand work from them – which brings up the topic of homework.

---

[71] Rudolf Steiner, *The Child's Changing Consciousness: As the Basis of Pedagogical Practice* (Anthroposophic Press, 1996), April 20, 1924, p. 141.

Homework

"When your children come home from school, we hope that you enjoy it when they talk about the things they enjoyed at school. We hope that you enjoy the joyous face of the children when they come home after school."[72]
~ Rudolf Steiner

THE IDEAL WOULD BE for students to *want* to continue their school work at home in some form or fashion, depending on what excites them. It was partly what Rudolf Steiner envisioned, and he said as much in various succinct statements, such as "...we also need to consider that the work done at home must be done happily. The children must feel a need to do it."[73] Or in one of the earlier faculty meetings with the teachers in Stuttgart, "I want to be perfectly clear that it is possible within the normal school day to achieve the ideal through rational work so that the children are spared tiring homework." But he did concede that "we must initiate a kind of modified homework. [...]

[But] we should be clear that we do not want to overburden them. They should not feel they are groaning under the weight of their homework. They need to do it happily, in which case assigning them a task has a genuinely good influence"[74] One should bear that in mind when assigning homework, no matter what grade.

There are good teachers who like to give a lot of homework, and there are good teachers who prefer to give none at all, or only on a voluntary basis. I recall a teacher in the Rudolf Steiner Schule Bochum, who did not believe in homework and made room for all the work to be done during the Main Lesson or in one of the middle-of-the-day classes. However, the teacher who taught the parallel class, was all for giving a great deal of homework from third grade on. It was interesting to note that in high school the teachers could not see any marked difference in the academic abilities between these two classes. They both fared well in high school. The question is: what do the children need, and how can I, as their teacher, make them enjoy and love school as much as possible? There are, however, some best practices and guidelines.

In my first and second grade I gave no formal homework, yet parents told me that their children would practice the letters of the alphabet at home, or enjoy drawing scenes from the fairytales they had heard. A number of the children (mostly girls) became teachers at home, teaching their dolls form drawing, knitting, writing, and other lessons they had heard in school. Or they would retell in great detail what they had covered in school (a form of recall). Of course, not all children do that, but most class teachers know about their students doing this voluntary homework. They were taking pure joy in the work. In that regard they were fulfilling Steiner's ideal vision of homework.

From third grade on I began to assign official homework, though I tried to make it interesting, playful, varied, and never too much. The children welcomed the homework. The emphasis was on awakening their curiosity, in trying to discover what was unique in the problems or questions I posed. As Steiner remarked, "We should make the children curious about their work. If you ask the children such questions, that makes them curious about what they can find out for themselves. That is something that will excite them."[75] I continued this rhythm, more or less, through the grades, and the homework became firmly entrenched in the weekly rhythm. Every Monday they would receive the homework, with assignments due on respective days during the week. The contents, of course, changed, depending on the prevailing Main Lesson, and the math homework was often dealt with during a class later in the day and not necessarily during Main Lesson. Some of the assignments were nevertheless voluntary, and I included extra homework for the especially eager and able students. Inevitably, the enthusiasm affected other students who then showed me their attempts with pride.

It is imperative to remain consequent when assigning obligatory homework. One can be lenient and modify the homework for certain students, but one should not let it go. Letting students "get away" with undone homework undermines the word and intentions of the teacher. Clarity around the issue of homework is essential. I find this to be especially pertinent in regard to homework in the high school. Steiner underscores this point: "One basic principle is that we know the children do the homework, and that we never find that they do not do it. You should never give children homework unless you know they will bring the solved problems back, and that they have done them with zeal. A liveliness needs to come into the work, and we need to encourage the children so that their inner attitude is not paralyzed." But he goes on to underscore the students' relationship to the homework. "You should bring it about that the children want to do what they need to do in school."[76] Easier said than done. It raises questions: do we think enough about the kind of homework we assign? Are we creative enough? Do we appeal to the students' curiosity, their eagerness, and leanings? Is it too much? Oftentimes we fall short.

Another consideration is whether the homework is truly essential and whether one can do it in the classroom. At the end of the section quoted above, Steiner reiterates: "Our goal must be to cover the material in such a way that we don't need anything outside of school."[77] This was easier to accomplish in the lower school, but not in the high school. It is almost impossible to get by without giving some homework in the high school. Important academic goals have to be met. It fosters independent work habits and nudges them to put their thoughts down on paper with clarity, which schools their thinking. Granted, it is more of a challenge for the teacher to come up with creative ideas that will spark their curiosity and speak to the students' interests. Giving choices is a great help. It addresses the students' leanings. Asking the students to come up with pertinent assignments in regard to the material has spawned some exciting results. However, giving the students too much freedom can potentially result in pitfalls.

I continued suggesting homework assignments in the lower grades that were purely voluntary, such as drawing a map from their home to the school during the local history and geography block. Then I would – as Steiner suggested – "wait and see if the children prepare the work at home."[78] Those kinds of assignments were almost always completed by all the students.

With mathematics I found it helpful for the students to figure out the problems themselves at home. Can they do the math problems without the help of the teacher or one of their friends? Nor did I mind if their parents or guardians helped them, because it also assured some together time (as long as the parents didn't do the work for them, purely for the sake of completing the task).

I rarely let the students take their Main Lesson books home because when I did it was often forgotten the next day. However, I always made exceptions with some students who

I could rely on, or if they had missed too many classes and had to catch up with some work. In these cases, it was always in conjunction with the parents.

As mentioned, most of the assignments in the lower grades are done during school, either during the Main Lesson or in one of the middle-of-the day classes. They support and enhance the curriculum, in accordance with the academic guidelines of each particular grade. They build a whole palette of skills, whether artistic or academic. Ask yourself: what will get them excited? What will help them deepen their understanding of the subject matter? Are they up to the task, or is it beyond them, or too simple? Are your instructions clear? This is especially true for the more academic assignments in middle or high school, such as research projects. They need clear outlines on how to proceed. Every assignment needs conscious preparation. Nothing is a given, because in many cases it is the first time that they are getting introduced to something, and inevitably instructions need to be repeated. This holds true in the high school as well (or even in college), when one has to repeat the rundown of a research project one more time. In other words: the teacher should strive to be crystal clear about what and why the work is assigned.

---

[72] Rudolf Steiner, *The Spirit of the Waldorf School: Lectures Surrounding the Founding of the First Waldorf School* (Anthroposophic Press, 1995), August 31, 1919, p. 66.
[73] Rudolf Steiner, *Faculty Meeting with Rudolf Steiner: Volume 2* (Anthroposophic Press, 1998), 12.9.1922, p. 474.
[74] Rudolf Steiner, *Faculty Meeting with Rudolf Steiner: Volume 1* (Anthroposophic Press, 1998), 6.21.1922, p. 364.
[75] Ibid. p. 335.
[76] Ibid p. 285.
[77] Ibid. p. 285.
[78] Ibid. p. 285.

Threats to the Main Lesson

"To overcome the hurdle, bring warmth into the lesson. Warmth, warmth!"[79] ~ Rudolf Steiner

ALREADY IN STEINER'S time teachers asked whether the children could start the day off with gymnastics or eurythmy. Steiner spoke against these suggestions, pointing out that the "children would then come to main lesson tired. They would be just as tired as if they had a regular period before main lesson."[80]

I am reiterating this point, because proposals to have movement classes before Main Lesson is brought up every now and then and also implemented in some schools. There are, of course, extenuating circumstances where that is unavoidable for any number of reasons. However, if it becomes the norm it implies that the essence of the Main Lesson is no longer understood in its full breadth and depth. The morning class is where "the child needs to exert forces of the *head*,"[81] for which it ought to be as receptive as possible, and anything that tires them out beforehand, such as a PE class, will impede optimal learning. Furthermore, the magic of the night echoes into this foundational lesson of the day. As the German saying goes: *Morgenstund hat Gold im Mund* – in other words: There is golden power in the morning hour. An invisible freshness hovers around the morning that is fragile and delicate. It can easily be disturbed and shooed away. But with poetry and song during the short rhythmical part it gets enlivened and invited in.

Nevertheless, in the high school one often has drowsy students lugging themselves to their desks, and one has to do some conscious conducting to get those cobwebs removed. And it's no secret that many of them have been up half the night watching movies, playing video games, or spent time with their devices in one way or another. Starting school much later is often suggested, which does not solve the most pressing concern: dealing with the social media.

Many of the students are overloaded with extracurricular activities and have little free time. Or they do not eat before coming to school, leaving them with low blood sugar, which can cause inattention and irritability, and generally undermines their learning potential. Academic success rests partly on a healthy breakfast. These points are beyond the immediate control of the teacher, though one can address them vigorously at parent evenings and private parent meetings. When students literally fall asleep in class it is best to observe it, then address it, either in a humorous manner, or after class in a quiet moment. Hearing from them what is going on usually puts things into context and one has something to work with. When they notice that you are not coming down on them, they feel seen and will often try to be more present, or they will take up your offer that they can put their head on the table (or even lie down in some cases). However, mostly they begin to wake up within the first ten minutes of singing, poetry, or other exercise, unless there is a pre-existing condition for which one makes allowances. And, to underscore, it often does not need much.

When a whole high school class feels weighed down, I have found that a guided 'meditation' helps them arrive and wake up, as counterintuitive as it may sound. Of course, it needs to fit into the thematic content the current block. For instance, during the *Parzival* block in 11th grade, I have led them through the "rice bowl" meditation, as I call it. Similarly to the Tibetan monks, who use the rice bowl as an object for meditation, I start off asking the juniors to imagine their own little rice bowl as vividly as possible: its weight, size, shape, how it feels to the fingers, the age, what it is made out of, and so forth. From there I lead them through a metamorphic sequence where the humble rice bowl is gradually transformed into a radiant grail, and then slowly back to the humble little rice bowl in their palms. It is a form of storytelling that addresses the ever-wakeful essence that we all share as humans.

The content, if presented imaginatively, has rejuvenating effects. Many students cannot help but get involved. Even if their bodies remain sluggish, the will in their minds is aroused. This triggered *will* warms and wakens them. As I draw them in through the content, they get drawn out of their personal fatigue. They respond to the ideals. Pictures, imaginations, feelings all help to stir the will. Something in the depths of their souls recognizes and responds to the content and overcomes their temporary temporal predicament. I have noticed the droopiest students wake up when hearing content to which they can relate. This enlivened, artistic, and potentized lesson, makes for a gentler, but more effective lesson that addresses as much as possible the whole human being. This is the true and life-filled "academic rigor" that needs to be pursued, which overcomes lethargy and apathy that so easily enters every realm of education in our materialistic and intellectual age.

In some cases, when parents (or the students themselves) claim that they are not met academically, what they really mean is that there was a lack of true content – that the learners weren't touched in the core of their being. If one includes the full measure of a well-rounded lesson that embraces meaningful content with broader perspectives, then the academic and intellectual aspects fall into place. It calls for *depth recognition* on the part of the teacher.

In many ways we are still in the throes of habits, customs, and traditions that go back hundreds of years and are the end result of intellectualism that has its roots in catechism, which devolved into an increasingly mechanized view of the world, supported by the materialistic-scientific mindset that displaced the human's eternal core being with the intellect – a necessary, but ultimately one sided surrogate. Europe's "classical" educational system has lost the mythological elements and become an empty mold, which in the long run can never satisfy the deeper needs of the evolving human being, no matter how clever and how hard it tries to hold on to its power. The result is a lopsided materialistic educational system that forces children to learn by rote rather than love.

Often those who criticize Waldorf education of being too Eurocentric, are actually the ones holding on most fiercely to the mechanistic strain of the European heritage, firmly based on intellectual learning conventions and traditions that tote exams, tests, and point systems, where the students are pitted against one another, and scrupulous competition and shameless ambitions is the order of the day. The critics will say: do we really need to study the European classics, the works of Homer, Dante, Shakespeare, Norse mythology, fairytales, and so forth? Shouldn't we have the students learn about marginalized and current writers? Indeed, we should, must and do. It's also essential to study modern literature that examines contemporary issues. We must include more women writers and people of color. But not at the exclusion of the world's great surviving mythology, which not only speaks to the deepest and most sublime core of the human condition, but contains *within it* the wisdom that precedes Europe, through Greece, Africa, Persia, all the way to Asia. And hearing and learning about them we hear about the creation of the world through the consciousness of all the different peoples of the world, no matter where –

because the story of creation is one and the same all over the earth, only it is told in fascinating variations.

The Main Lesson is a concept that, interestingly enough, is gaining traction in many other schools, where there is a recognition of working in blocks, and of having more time devoted to one subject. Yet, the irony is that in Waldorf Schools we notice an increasing tendency to become more fragmented, to divide the day into shortened sections, including the Main Lesson. If the Main Lesson starts to lose its signature place in the day, then Waldorf education will lose its life forces and be unable to manifest the grand renewal of education that Rudolf Steiner envisioned for our modern times, stretching far into the future. The "veritable child of care" will have succumbed, which Steiner warned against right from at the outset in 1919.

Another threat is the increasing trend toward *specialization*, even in the lower school. It is part and parcel of the tendency to limit the looping of the class teacher and having more and more specialists come into the middle school during Main Lesson. Or forcing the teachers to adhere to certain methods of teaching that are not steeped in the Waldorf approach, even if they share some parallel aspects. The Waldorf method is not quite trusted anymore. Proponents of "keeping up with the times," will concede that Waldorf is "nice" and "artistic," but will argue that the children now really need something more rigorous and down to earth. And so, we introduce Orton-Gillingham method or the Singapore approach to Mathematics. There is nothing wrong with that, per se. On the contrary, both of these approaches are helpful and excellent in many ways, and there are certainly overlaps, but I have seen and observed how they are used at the expense of deepening and understanding the Waldorf approach. Furthermore, the suggestions that Steiner gave, and the resultant research that many Waldorf teachers have explored and implemented – and still needs to be continued – is subsequently ignored, forgotten, or dismissed. When Steiner says "that we often forget that we have a different method and a different curriculum than in other schools,"[82] he was lamenting the fact that his innovative guidelines were not furthered, developed, or adhered to and that the teachers were falling back into old modes of teaching, based on their own education. At the same December 9th faculty meeting in 1922, he goes on to say: "The question we need to ask ourselves is whether we are unconsciously not using the Waldorf method where we have not achieved results."[83] Though he recognized that some of the results are "uneven," he wanted the teachers to continue exploring the new guidelines: "You get the results when you use the methods. [...] In arithmetic I have the feeling that the Waldorf School method is not often used."[84] What is worrisome is that when we increasingly forego Waldorf methods, we forget what they stand for and why they were suggested in the first place. More importantly, it thwarts new research based on Steiner's indications, which would meet the changing times. That said, I have been pleased to see how some teachers have become even more excited about teaching in a more in-depth Waldorf way out of anthroposophy after taking a 'new approach' training session. Others are successfully combining the various methods creatively.

It is expedient to review the curriculum periodically. However, it is occasionally seen as a way to get rid of subjects perceived as no longer relevant, such as *Parzival* or Goethe's *Faust*, the Romantics or Shakespeare – literature written by *dead white European men*. But instead of getting rid of these blocks in the high school, one should rather reexamine why they were introduced in the first place, what their importance is in world evolution, and what place they hold in the "consciousness age." *How* one teaches and *why* one teaches that specific content – that is what should be reviewed. Based on the results, we can adjust the teaching style to make it relevant. Whatever we teach *must remain relevant and accessible*. Though there are some things which we might choose forego, it is self-evident that we need to present the content differently nowadays. With this in mind, I began my last block on Goethe's *Faust* with the words: "You might ask yourselves why we are studying a work of literature by a rich white male, long deceased, from Europe." One student of color immediately remarked, "Yes, good question, why?" And so, I gave a short answer of justification, and promised to keep the "universal themes" as germane as possible throughout the block, and I urged them to put me on the spot should the content get too "stuffy" and irrelevant in any way.

Goethe spent most of his life writing *Faust*, which deals with the question of evil and knowledge. Though one could say that evil has been with humanity from the beginning (one just needs to refer to mythology from around the world, including Adam and Eve), the effects are everywhere. In times past, people could still escape it, like the Essenes (Judaic sect that existed between the 2nd century BCE and the end of the 1st century CE) or the hermits and holy people around the world, but nowadays the detrimental effects caused by humanity are irrevocably felt in all parts of the earth in the form of pollution, radiation, and natural imbalances caused by exploitation of natural resources, to name only a few examples. There is no escaping the "evils" anymore. Goethe's *Faust*, although set in the middle ages, touches on almost all manifestations of "evil." The "deal with the devil" is all around us. As modern human beings we cannot help but be complicit in some way. The Faustian question is alluded to in thousands of films, TV shows, plays, novels, and newspaper articles, directly and indirectly. The "hot" and "cold" evil, embodied by Mephisto, lives in us as it does in the world. Studying *Faust* brings this to consciousness. It offers clues to the *Riddle of Evil*, which we, as humanity, need to solve, step for conscious step. The way Faust treats Gretchen alone is an example of sexual harassment, which is starting to be exposed through the "me too" movement. No other masterpiece of literature addresses the subject of evil as comprehensively as Gothe's *Faust*. The same holds true with other great works, including the Transcendentalists, Homer, or Eschenbach's *Parzival.*

At the end of the *Faust* block, I got an email from the girl's mother of the student who'd said, "Yes, good question, why?" at the beginning of the block. The email read: "It's been an honor & privilege for A__ to have been under your tutelage. With every day spent with you, she came home exhilarated & engaged!" And three years earlier the students from the senior class insisted that we perform *Faust* for their senior play (They also insisted that Mephisto be female). They recognized its significance in our time. And that was a class that was comprised of about ten nationalities with diverse racial and religious backgrounds, and varied gender identifications.

With the tremendous growth of Waldorf schools, the attacks have increased accordingly. That is natural. What is more disconcerting, however, are the criticisms from within the movement. We see a growing trend of Waldorf schools and/or teachers trying to cuddle up to mainstream norms, the very norms that so many teachers within the public-school system (and private school sector) are decrying and rebelling against. This can lead to a superficiality and mainstreaming of Waldorf education. And because there is a dire shortage of teachers, we have an increasing number who are hired without any training whatsoever (especially in the high school, but not exclusively), or who are sympathetic to some aspects of Waldorf education, but not to the deeper layers. Amongst them there are excellent teachers in their own right, but they lack the connection to Steiner's indications and have little interest to arrive at a fuller understanding of why we do what we do. This can cause conflicts when these teachers come into leadership positions. Sadly, teachers who work out of anthroposophy run the risk of being sidelined. By the same token, some diehard Waldorf teachers can be too dogmatic and inflexible, unable to keep up with the rapidly changing world. And schools that go by "Steiner Schools" change their names, and if the logo seems too "anthroposophical," conventional graphic designers are hired with no connection to the spiritual underpinnings, who come up with depictions that miss the true artistic essence of the education. Why, we might ask? But one of the greatest threats to the Main Lesson and the Waldorf movement as such, is the increasing reliance on *media*, distance learning, and online education. The lockdown due to Covid 19 has made that abundantly clear in all sectors of education, as all of us have had to give online classes and attend Zoom meetings. Educators around the planet have pointed out the obvious negative effects of online courses. Granted, there are, as with all things, some beneficial aspects to online learning, but the negatives far outweigh the positives, especially in Waldorf education, which is based on face-to-face learning. That said, this burning topic goes beyond the scope of this chapter and needs a separate article or book in which properly to address the details of this pressing issue.

Not only do we need to keep abreast of the times, but more importantly, we need to be *ahead* of the times. It is essential to intuit what is coming toward us. Furthermore, it is incumbent on us to continue being trailblazers in the realm of education. If we remove Rudolf Steiner from the Waldorf movement, or hide the spiritual underpinnings, we are, in essence, plucking the flower, leaving it to wilt. Instead, we should care for the soil and let the plant grow and flourish. Like the plant, Waldorf education needs to be intimately and firmly connected to its roots if any rejuvenation and renewal is to take place.

---

[79] Rudolf Steiner, *Rudolf Steiner Konferenzen mit den Lehrern der Freien Waldorfschule in Stuttgart: Erste Band.* Translated by Eric G. Müller (Dornach: Rudolf Steiner Verlag, GA 300/1, 1975), 15.11. 1920, p. 238.
[80] Steiner, *Faculty Meeting with Rudolf Steiner: Volume 2*, p. 472.
[81] Rudolf Steiner, *Discussion with Teachers*, p. 19.
[82] Rudolf Steiner, *Faculty Meeting with Rudolf Steiner: Volume 2*, p. 474.
[83] Ibid.
[84] Ibid.

Preparing for the Main Lesson

"In life it is not the ready-made knowledge that has value, but the work that leads to this knowledge, and particularly in the art of education this work has its own special value."[85] ~ Rudolf Steiner

IN LECTURE ONE OF *Balance in Teaching,* Rudolf Steiner says, "At the end of the school year you say, yes only now can I do what I ought to have been doing. This is a very real feeling! And hiding within it is a certain secret. If at the beginning of the school year you had really been able to do all you could do at the end, you would have taught badly. You have good lessons because you had to work them out as you went along!"[86]

As a class teacher I certainly experienced that feeling of inadequacy not only at the end of every year, but at the end of every Main Lesson block. Most Waldorf teachers have the same experience. One wishes one could immediately start over again – this time with fewer mistakes and awkward moments, while the content is still fresh. Only at the end of a block does one really understand what one should have done. As teachers we are always scrutinizing ourselves, questioning what worked, what didn't, where the lessons fell short, the areas that needed improvement, and what should have been left out or added. One has finally arrived at the right rhythm and flow of the block. The enthusiasm and excitement still echo on. The notion that it is normal – even positive – to have this sense of insufficiency has been of little comfort to me. The knowledge that one could have and should have done better is real and leaves a bitter aftertaste. However, at least one can say with certainty: I have learned the most during this block. True, the students were exposed to my struggle and ongoing effort, but the next block is already waiting, and I find myself once again trembling at the thought and doubting my abilities. And so, in the earnest attempt to alleviate our fears, we *prepare*, we put in the effort. And though it won't dispel the self-doubt (no matter how much we prepare), it does supply a healthy foundation. You are giving the students something.

Preparing for any class is central to a teacher's vocation. And one has to distinguish between two types of preparation, though they merge together and form a whole. First, we prepare the actual subject matter as outlined in the curriculum. The second is more peripheral in nature in that it encompasses the more universal aspects, informing us, for instance, *how* it might fit into the overall development of the child, or how the respective subject matter is connected to the human being. Furthermore, our syllabus also includes elements dictated by cultural conventions, even though they might not be beneficial to children of a certain age, such as the abundance of abstractions we are expected to teach to the very young, and some theoretical hypotheses to the older students, which are important to know because they are part of our modern culture. Our age, for example, still insists on calling the heart a pump, and teaches it as if it were, yet, one only needs to follow phenomena based scientific data to understand that the heart is not a pump, though it seems to have pump like qualities[87]. We then have to find ways of introducing the material so that it is nevertheless imbued with unbiased observation and living imaginations, just as we do when teaching the abstract letters in first grade artistically, through stories and pictures. In like manner we approach the various scientific theories, such as Newton's color theory versus Goethe's, or the Big Bang theory. Sometimes we get so used to these conventions that we do not question or reevaluate them for the sake of pedagogical relevance.

Steiner indicated that every hour of teaching requires three hours of preparation. Preparation takes many forms, and the kind of preparation needed depends on the teacher, the relationship to the material, the class, and the individual children. Finding the right relationship to the material fuels excitement, as does the idea of presenting something new to the children – love for the content and love for the students makes preparation fulfilling. It doesn't always come easy and one has to overcome oneself. At other times it's like riding a wave. Outer and inner circumstances play a role. Either way, we have to put in a great deal of effort!

It is a common experience to feel underprepared – those days when one has literally had no time to prepare, like after a late-night faculty or College meeting. In this case, a quick, sharp, and condensed five-minute focus on the contents of the lesson can help. Funnily enough, those lessons often turn out better than expected. Teachers do receive a lot of grace, but grace cannot be relied upon. Time is a flexible thing; it defies time itself. Even if we *have* prepared for hours, it still doesn't guarantee a thriving lesson. Obviously, the students have to learn something, but so much depends on *how* we teach and whether our teaching is lively enough to animate the children, which begs the question: Does the content enliven *us*? Do we feel the joy, the passion?

We've all had days when we've bumbled through a Main Lesson, felt overcome by guilt, recognized that it was far from perfect, only to go home and be inundated with a slew of unexpected good ideas on how to proceed. Occasionally, we need "bum" classes in order to get going again, to find a new rhythm, and to latch on to previous preparations that had gone dormant and were forgotten.

One needs to distinguish between the daily preparations during the block, and the general planning before the beginning of the block. One has to allow ample time for preparations, which then permits for all sorts of experiences to suddenly become relevant to the subject matter in question. Both are essential. If one relies solely on the more immediate preparation done the day or two before, then it won't have had enough gestation time, or it might not fit harmoniously enough within the context of the whole block. Good ideas need time to grow, and if granted, the larger context will not be lost. Conversely, if one prepares diligently ahead of the block and barely anything during the actual block, one is likely to forget many aspects and run the risk of not offering enough with fresh vibrancy. Combined, the three-hour prep rule for one hour of teaching holds true. Altogether, it usually ends up being more than three hours. The following suggestions and guidelines have been helpful for me:

It is a good practice to determine what is needed and what you will have to teach during the upcoming school year, methodically. And each grade and subject have different requirements and parameters. Ensure that you get a thorough overview of the year. Once that is clarified, a well-balanced schedule can be constructed. Some blocks lend themselves more to a specific season, such as the 5th grade Botany block that is best taught during Spring or Fall, or both. Once the schedule of the year is more or less clear (there are always unforeseen events or circumstances, which will justify adjustments in the yearly schedule) one can get a head start on the preliminary reading, which for me was the most enjoyable part, because I could already imagine teaching the content to the class while engrossed in the material, and it fired my excitement. Every subject and every grade has something to get enthusiastic about.

In first grade I immersed myself in fairytales, reading as many as I could, without making any specific choices, though I made a list of preferred tales. What a treat! Not only the fairytales as such, but finding the soul-spiritual significance within the fairytales. This is especially important because in our global age we need to go further afield and choose folk tales from around the world, without, of course, discarding the Grimm's fairytales, and their profound use of archetypes, especially for our Consciousness Soul Age, as we go forward into an ever more challenging future. In this regard, the teacher must acquire an in-depth connection to the contents of the story. She has to experience deeply within herself what lives in these stories as moral virtues and their innate transformative power. The retelling of these fairytales, myths, or legends, will then be profoundly imbued with their grand gifts, their medicinal power. This needs to be experientially underscored, because of the current misunderstanding of so many fairytales and myths, due to an overly intellectual approach. Once we have discovered their implicit power, we will find warmth-filled words that will allow the children to feel the full impact of the "deep, dark forest," the "seven mountains and seven valleys" that first had to be crossed, and all the other archetypes and imponderables of these rich stories.

This holds true for every subject: *what* we teach depends on *how* and *why* we teach (my ongoing mantra). And oftentimes it requires us to forego our personal prejudices, or those that are currently in vogue, and objectively enter into the living pictures to intimate their intrinsic value.

In second grade I spent the summer immersed in the lives of holy people and Saints from around the world, and also animal stories and fables. In the higher grades the reading becomes more demanding, especially regarding history or the sciences. Getting acquainted with the curriculum helps in the planning of the optimal block schedule for the year.

The more I read and prepared for the upcoming school year, the more enthusiastic I became. I couldn't wait to impart the knowledge, even though it often proved more difficult in reality to get the material across successfully. The long American summer recess allows for a lengthy gestation period. Many teachers even plan their vacations accordingly. A teacher from our school planned an Italy trip before sixth grade, which helped him enter into the mood of the ancient Romans. Another teacher embarked on a cross country trip before the fifth grade, readying herself for the American geography block. Likewise, it became the norm for me to imagine all of my students accompanying me on my sundry travels; and I'd point out this or that, giving them imaginary lessons. These mental lessons were later embodied in the actual Main Lessons during the year. Once you become a class teacher, the students are always with you in one way or another. This is also true for high school teachers, although not quite so exclusively. I consciously journeyed to

Troy because of my Homer blocks, and visited Epidaurus and other amphitheaters for my Tragedy & Comedy class. Other trips related to the curriculum included a visit to the rocky and steep cliff'd village of Caltabellotta in Sicily to get a feel for the alleged landscape of Klingsor, the evil ruler that caused the imprisonment of the 400 ladies in the Castle of Wonders found in the Eschenbach's *Parzival*; the Goethe Haus in Frankfurt; and numerous places that related to my History through Music class. In fact, any and all places become relevant to one's teaching. It adds meaning and intentionality to the summer vacation. It even works in reverse. Many years after teaching the Voyages of Discovery, my wife and I traveled to Portugal and made a pilgrimage to the promontory of Cape Sagres where Henry the Navigator lived, founded, and developed a school of navigation, and where captains and seafaring men were prepared for what they might encounter on their voyages into the unknown. I found myself talking inwardly to my old class in Eugene, just as I had many years before as their class teacher.

One of my most enjoyable preparations was before my astronomy class. I only knew the rudiments of the fixed stars, the zodiac, and the planets, though I always had a healthy and reverent awe of the night sky. Here was my opportunity. It took me a while to get truly acquainted with the constellations and to observe the movements of the starry firmament, and I was grateful that I had the summer to prepare myself.

Even so, some blocks need extra preparation time during the school year, especially if they demand a great deal of equipment and set up. I would consciously place them after one of the short vacations, such as spring break, or a long weekend. And I made a point of sandwiching these more work intensive blocks between blocks that came more easily to me.

What proved helpful, and gave me the most peace of mind was soliciting the advice of other class teachers who had taught the respective blocks before. I would seek out at least two experienced teachers and ask for their counsel: how they had built up their lessons, what they found important, their understanding of the material, and what class activities they found interesting and successful. Invariably, I returned from these "counseling sessions" with armfuls of books. I cannot underscore the value those meetings afforded me. It truly gave me not only the confidence to enter into the Main Lesson, but it triggered my excitement. I did not necessarily follow their example, but I always gained something significant and important from them. We can learn from everybody.

In this regard I would also like to mention the teacher conferences. Whenever I went to a regional or national conference, I made a point of getting together with other teachers who were teaching the same grade, asking them what, when, and how they were teaching the various blocks. In some conferences these meetings were consciously scheduled in advance.

To this day there is something cleansing about clearing away the piles of books, papers, or equipment after a Main Lesson block, and getting ready for a new subject, with another set of books and papers. As a class teacher I usually changed my classroom slightly, which would highlight the new material in some form or other, by either adding or removing pictures on the wall, or changing the nature table, making an introductory blackboard drawing, or altering the seating arrangement.

And still, with all of that, I often felt as if I was only a day or two ahead of the class in my preparations. No matter how much reading I did, or if I have taught the subject before (as with my current high school blocks), I still find myself feeling rushed and not sufficiently prepared. On the other hand, whenever I am in the classroom, I have plenty to say and do with the students that I inevitably run out of time.

Still, every day is different, and one can never be quite sure of how the lesson will go. One way to counteract the unforeseen events that tend to occur when you least expect them (fire drills, surprise visitors, weather delay, lice inspection, absenteeism, socio-political events, tragedies, etc.) is to have different options available. It is always prudent to have extra provisions in the backpack. You might come to class and while standing in front of the students realize that you need to change course and teach another lesson. Having come to class with one intention and opting to go with another is not uncommon. And it is not necessarily the subject matter that one changes, but the approach – *how* one had planned to teach the lesson. Conversely, I have regretted sticking with a lesson plan, knowing I would have fared better by choosing something different. As always, it is a matter of remaining flexible, being open to changes, and practicing spontaneity. In other words: choosing the middle path between form and freedom.

When Steiner asks us to "read the children" he is asking us to glean directly from the students what is needed. "Reading" their needs will influence us in how we prepare, in how we teach, and in some instances, what we teach – especially in our more global times where we need to school and practice our sensitivities regarding the nuances of race, gender, religion, politics, and so forth. Our preparation is affected by who we have in our classes. When, for a few years, we had students from Afghanistan or Palestine in our school, I consciously made an effort in my preparations to know more about those cultures, which I subsequently included into the thematic content.

Timing plays an important role, and through thoughtful preparation one can be more in control of how the Main Lessons proceed. Most teachers endure the painful experience of not covering all they wanted to cover. At the beginning of a block one is under the illusion of having ample time, only to find that the block is already coming to an end and there is still so much to cover. This can also result in the teacher extending the course, with the consequence that the following block is truncated, or –

if it has happened on a number of occasions – a block might not be taught at all, something that happens more often than one might assume.

The focus on the overall arc of the block should be balanced out and spiced with a suitable amount of details, such as what drawings to include, choice of poems, written assignments, anecdotes, tangential stories, field trips, projects, grammar and new vocabulary. Each block lends itself to the introduction of new words. Alone, picking these words can be an artistic process, based on patterns, unique spelling, interesting etymology, such as the word "hieroglyphs" meaning "sacred carving" (Greek: *hieros* meaning "sacred" and *glyphein* meaning "to carve"). The vocabulary then has a context from which they learn the word and the spelling. This also holds true for correct grammar usage that one weaves into the lessons. If one has taught the difference between the active and passive voice in 6th grade, then one can make conscious use of active or passive sentences while teaching history, geography, or geology.

Conscious use of details becomes especially pertinent in the science classes. You need to know what equipment is needed for what experiment and have them ready. This needs double and triple checking. You might have everything in place, except for one important chemical that you forgot on the kitchen counter at home. I have to admit that even now, with careful planning and getting my "stuff" together, I still find myself wasting class time looking for something that I was convinced I had packed (or often have packed), but misplaced. As for technology: it has a way of not working when you need it most. Double checking pays off.

Steiner encourages the teachers to teach in the most living and fluid manner as possible, which means – *no notes*. Our preparations ought to be so thorough that we don't need notes, that we've made the subject matter our own, thoroughly. We must become the subject matter and relate to it with our whole being, so that the children can relate to it with their whole being. Steiner alludes to it in various lectures, but underscores this point in the introduction to the faculty meeting on February 6, 1923 in Stuttgart. "If a teacher needs to look at prepared notes to see what to do, the necessary contact with the students is interrupted. That should never occur. That is the ideal."[88] It is an ideal that over 100 years later teachers still fall short on. I have frequently observed that there is a music stand (often nicely draped with silks) between the students and the teacher on which there are notes or a book, to which the teacher refers to repeatedly. However, the stand between the teacher and the children functions as a visible obstruction, a barrier. It implies that we don't really know our material, so why should they? Of course, in some instances, we all need reminders. But does it become a habit and how often does it occur? I always feel slightly guilty when I find myself unsure of a certain fact, requiring me to quickly refer to my notes. It clearly interrupts the flow, especially when I have to shuffle through papers to find the right one. It's not bad, but not ideal. And sometimes I promise to come back to that point the next day – a promise that should to be kept.

Then there is an aspect that is subtler and more difficult to consciously prepare for, and that is *humor.* Humor works better if it arises out of the artistic organic arc of the main lesson. Humor brings levity to the class, balancing out the gravity of the more serious content. The students need both: humor and tragedy, the two fundamental human emotions, but especially humor because there is anyway so much in life that weighs people down. Steiner brings up humor in many of his pedagogical lectures, stressing its importance. He also addresses it during the February 6th faculty meeting mentioned above. Elements of happiness and sadness need to become part and parcel of all lessons, especially during the lengthy morning class. Through the levity of humor, the children get drawn out of themselves, whereas a poignant story or anecdote causes them to retreat into themselves. The best humor comes through the natural flow of the Main

Lesson. Unplanned humor has the best punch. It arises out of the moment, which does dependent on who you are, your temperament, the rapport you have with the students, and the freedom with which you work with the material. Maybe the best, funniest, and lightest part of the lesson happens when you go off on a tangent that has organically presented itself. However, if you do have difficulties in bringing humor to the class, it is possible to plan and structure a lesson accordingly. Knowing that the students will have been working seriously for the whole main lesson, then Steiner urges that you "try to at least tell some funny story at the end of the period. [...] That is very necessary."[89] It will transform the mood into one of satisfied levity.

If we bear the whole child in mind and prepare accordingly, then we have come closer to the ideal.

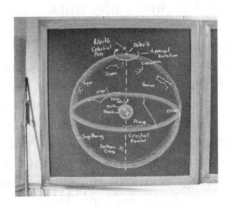

[85] Rudolf Steiner, *Balance in Teaching* (Anthroposophic Press, 2007), 9. 15. 1923, p. 9.

[86] Rudolf Steiner, *Balance in Teaching* (Anthroposophic Press, 2007), 9. 15. 1923, p. 8

[87] See Craig Holdrege (Ed.), *The Dynamic Heart and Circulation*, (Fair Oaks: AWSNA, 2002)

[88] Rudolf Steiner, *Faculty Meeting with Rudolf Steiner: Volume 2* (Anthroposophic Press, 1998), 2.6.1923, p. 540.

[89] Rudolf Steiner, *Faculty Meetings with Rudolf Steiner: Volume 2* (Anthroposophic Press, 1998), p. 539

Storytelling

"What was in his face showed that he was ready to respond to and make articulate the rhythm of the night. He was a storyteller because he was attuned to this rhythm and had in his memory the often repeated incidents that would fit it... [...] A real faith in human powers is present."[90]
~ Padraic Colum

ONE OF THE MOST important prerequisites of a teacher is the ability to tell stories. Storytelling is an art that needs cultivation and practice. Storytelling is at the core of successful teaching because it implicitly includes the highest educational ideals. It is the Waldorf teachers' greatest tool. This holds true for teaching first graders, seniors, and all the grades in between. Teachers are, in essence, storytellers and need to aspire toward becoming master storytellers. Yes, we can give instructions, we can do power point presentations, we can ask the students to open up their books and read certain passages, or give them handouts followed by questionnaires that test their comprehension. But that is not the lifeblood of teaching, though it has its place. There is enough evidence that mere instructing makes it more difficult for students to retain and remember information, let alone glean deeper insights, the more imponderable meanings.

In the lower grades the children listen to fairytales, fables, and mythologies from around the world. But it does not end there. No matter what subject, the development of the lessons adheres to the same kind of lawfulness that is contained in storytelling. On a rudimentary level stories demand vibrant and imaginative retelling, clarity of speech, clear introductions, logical development, and succinct conclusions. These exact attributes are essential in all teaching, no matter what discipline, what subject. Making use of pictures will help to clarify aspects that are difficult to put into words, especially when one tries to impart qualities. It demands clarity of thought and cogent use of language, enhanced through similes and metaphors, whether one teaches the humanities, the sciences, a music or math class. All teachers know that concepts, theories, ideas – whatever they are – need to be explained in different ways in order for students to 'get it.' If they don't understand something, change the narrative!

Part of the ancient Celtic storytellers' training was under the tutelage of Druids. And likewise, the Druids had to master the art of storytelling from master bards. Their wisdom tales spread the word amongst the people, kept customs and traditions alive, spread news, and imparted important lessons. The same is true for the troubadours, the trouvéres, the African Griots, the ancient Greek rhapsodes, and the eastern and Native American shamans. In essence, all spiritual leaders of the past were tellers of wisdom tales. They were all considered to be healers and spiritual teachers. And in truth, as teachers we are also healers and protectors. Each age has its discomforts and crises. And students entering our classroom have their individual ailments and inner turmoil that are in need of healing. We live in troubled times. As teachers we see it daily. If we take teaching seriously, we know that teaching is so much more than imparting knowledge. We are helping them to become the best they can be, humbly supplying stepping stones to facilitate their paths towards freedom. And our lessons, our storytelling helps to lead them to themselves. The more we become cognizant of this responsibility, the more we will awaken to the importance of working on the art of storytelling. We have to become like Scheherazade who administers her nightly stories to the wounds of her husband Shahryar, helping to transform and heal him of his own ill-digested pain.

Especially in the kindergarten and the first few grades teachers are encouraged to tell "pedagogical stories" to help specific children or a group of children to overcome certain discomforts or challenges. One might be skeptical, as I initially was. But I soon learned the power of stories, how they can have an almost magical effect; how behavior can change, sometimes overnight, though follow up stories are needed to support the remedial results, just like Scheherazade had to continue telling her story to King Shahryar. One could say that Waldorf education is one big story over a period of 12 years.

Of the thousands of accounts that highlight the power of stories I will give two moving and telling examples. In a short essay Nigerian author Chinua Achebe, who wrote *Things Fall Apart*, refers back to an incident that occurred when he first came to America in 1972 and was living in Amherst, Massachusetts. He had to bring his daughter, Nwando, to a nursery school, but she did not want to go and hated it. Every day when he dropped her off at the preschool, Wonderhaven, she cried pitifully. Furthermore, he was told that she refused to say a single word all day long in the kindergarten, preferring to sit alone and silent, feeling "desolate." He did not know what to do when he suddenly had an idea. After weeks and weeks of helplessly witnessing his poor daughter's tears, he finally made a deal with her, promising to tell her a story while driving to school if she promised to stop crying. Nwando agreed. True to his word he told her a story every morning on the way to school and she didn't cry when he dropped her off. After a while he noticed that when he came to fetch her at the end of the day, she would add another story on the way back. Not only that, but he learned from the kindergarten teacher that she would tell stories to the other children in the class. The problem had been solved! The story sustained her, and in turn she entertained the others in that kindergarten with stories, so much so that her classmates called the school "Nwanda-haven," instead of Wonderhaven.[91] Stories are powerful. Stories heal. Stories bring people together.

The remarkable book *Stolen Lives* by Malika Oufkir tells the true story of her entire family's 20-year imprisonment in Morocco after her father had plotted to assassinate the King. It was a dire situation and after ten years the strain had become sheer unbearable. That's when Malika had a "brainwave," as she put it:

> I was going to tell them a story. In this way I could talk to them about life, of love. I would give the younger ones the benefit of my experience; I would take them on journeys, and make them dream and laugh and cry. I would teach them history and geography, science and literature, I would give them everything I knew, and for the rest, well I'd improvise...[92]

The never-ending story she compiled about a Russian prince was called "The Black Flakes" and she told it to her five younger sisters and brothers over a period of ten years until the moment of their escape, aptly likening herself to Scheherazade. She took into account every one of their individual dispositions, their ages, struggles, and inner needs, always endeavoring to cloak the ongoing tale with life lessons in the most interesting and pictorial manner. Malika is convinced that the story and the characters saved them, that they otherwise would not have survived the ordeal, and that it kept them from going mad. This experience so closely mirrors what Waldorf teachers are trying to accomplish on a daily level. When it was all over, Malika wondered how on earth she could have come up with such a story, filled with intense and vivid details. "I don't know how my imagination managed to produce something like that and keep it going for those ten years without my ever tiring or boring my audience."[93] I suspect that "heaven" had something to do with it. That can be a great consolation to all Waldorf teachers because it confirms that we have the creative power deep within us – the will to imagine when the need arises. In the beginning was the word. Stories are spoken power-words. We just have to begin and then the ideas start flowing.

Speech: The importance of speech has already been mentioned numerous times, but we have to ask ourselves if we work sufficiently enough on our own speech. We recall how Rudolf Steiner, halfway through his brief 14-day teacher training course for the teachers of the first Waldorf school, began introducing speech exercises, highlighting the importance of speech. He was quite relentless, wanting the teachers to continue the speech work by themselves and in the pedagogical meetings.

Speech is emphasized in the various teacher training institutes, but it is not enough. It calls for ongoing practice. The children are formed through our voices. The teacher's voice influences the students also on a physical level. The larynx automatically copies everything it hears in its surroundings. It subtly imitates all sounds. This formative force changes the way children speak. So, it stands to reason that as teachers we must put the best voice forward.

Storytelling is an age-old oral tradition. It is the bearer of the first literature. And it is never only the story that the children hear. They hear and absorb the invisible, which help them form their own rich imaginations. They implicitly absorb the underlying morality contained in the story. But more than that, they "hear" how the deeper meanings are understood, penetrated, and lived by the teacher. All of the great literature of the world, including the folk tales, contain soul-spiritual aspects. If the teacher has consciously tried to pierce down through into the deepest layers of the stories, then something different will emerge and radiate in the telling. Apart from that, the children will be affected by the kind of person you are. It makes a difference whether a teacher is actively pursuing inner self development or not. We often hear of rigor, strict academic goals, measurable benchmarks, the testing of information, and so forth, but very little of these more imponderable aspects. How we tell the story will also influence how they will tell their own internal narrative to themselves as they go through life. Every story can be told in different ways. How are they going to tell their own story?

We get to know what we know by *telling* what we know, just as we can ascertain what we know when we put it down on paper. However, it is preceded by *hearing* the story, which contains the knowledge, the truth, the information. Odysseus first heard his own story told by the blind Phaeacian harpist, Demodocus. Through hearing the story of the Trojan War, including the vital role of the wooden horse, his understanding is prodded by being confronted by his own actions. This self-reflection is deepened when he is called upon to retell his own adventures to the Phaeacians, which helps him to fully understand what he had gone through. Whenever we come to this part of our study of Homer's *Odyssey* I am always moved by this moment when he *reveals* his identity, which is closely related to *hearing* his story and then *retelling* the rest of it. It is an essential step toward his self-development, proving the growth of his individuality. The story serves as a self-confrontation, enabling him to look at himself and his actions objectively. It strengthens and readies his "I," which earns him the trust of King Alcinous and Queen Arete (especially her) and a free passage back home to Ithaka. Only now, after ten long years of struggling to return home, is he strong and insightful enough to overcome the suitors, to reunite with Penelope –

his higher self – and to regain his sovereignty. But first he needed to know his own story before he could attain his goal, overcome the adversaries, and find his true self.

As all writers know, once they have written down their story, they need to adhere to three rules: rewrite, rewrite, rewrite. So, it goes with stories: perfecting the art of storytelling only happens through ongoing storytelling. The ancient Celtic storytellers had to climb multiple rungs on the ladder of storytelling under the rigorous supervision of a master storyteller for about 12 years.

We should never be daunted by the task. On the contrary – excited! Children are forgiving. We offer them our best, knowing we can always do better. Through imaginative pictures and a riveting plot, the story told by an experienced storyteller (teacher) engenders wonder, and wonder is the foundation of all learning, or to quote Thomas Aquinas, "Wonder is the desire for knowledge."

As we tell our stories (i.e. teach) we can gauge how the students listen. We listen to the quality of their listening, which informs us how we might continue. Each story is like a river. As we navigate down the story stream, we might steer a little to the right or left, or be led by the current here or there. We get an immediate and direct sense of how our story is coming across, if what we are saying is having the desired results. We sense whether we should wake them up slightly, calm them down, or bring the story to a close. Storytelling, like so much in life, is a two-way process. An astute storyteller always remains in charge, while staying awake to what lives in the audience.

Like the Greek rhapsode or Celtic bard, we need to put in our time, pay our dues, before we can call ourselves storytellers. Most of us start out as dilettantes and learn our trade on the job. Though it might come easy to some people (humans are storytellers by nature), it is quite another thing to deliver what is required for a teacher, where every word counts, even when we are not telling a story or presenting new material. We spend many hours a day talking to the students, and our speech must conform to all and every circumstance with a storyteller's sensitivity. Each one of us has to discover areas that need work. How is our enunciation and articulation? Do we struggle with volume? Are our voices too high or low, breathy or sharp, gravelly or screechy? Is our speech shallow and thin? Do our voices tire easily and become hoarse? Do we have a slight lisp or speech defect? Are we aware of phrasing and dynamics, or oblivious that we speak in a monotone? Do we tend to mispronounce words? Do we have an accent or dialect? Do we mumble through our words, have a drawl, or speak nasally? Do we mix metaphors, use incorrect or clumsy syntax? The list goes on.

Can we remember stories? Are we capable of clearly imagining everything we say? Do we have a sense for details? Do we inwardly see, hear, smell, and sense the contents of the story with all of our "twelve" senses, along with the sense of humor? Are we versatile enough to change our voice depending on the content? Are we clear about the story's geography? Can we read the children while telling the story, know whether to slow down or speed up, assess whether they are still with us? Can we be spontaneous and improvise? Can we feel ourselves into the age group, especially as a class teacher, where they change each year as they age? Is our speaking instrument saturated with life – the lips, larynx, tongue, palate – so that the refined and formed sound can free itself from the organs and be carried by our controlled breath through the air to the expectant and attentively listening children? Have we schooled ourselves in the art of fluidly sculpted sentences? Can we weave the sentences together into a molded whole? Can we enter into the genius of the language? The answer to all these questions is unequivocally, "Yes," but not without practice and daily doing. Not without love for the sounds and beauty of the language – the vehicle for truth and goodness. Not without entering deeply into the collective world cauldron of restorative stories.

I recall one student in our teacher education program who struggled to simply remember the story. It was an almost insurmountable hurdle, making it difficult for him to work on any of the other elements of storytelling. He mapped out the story, made drawings, wrote them out, read them aloud repeatedly, practiced with his wife and in front of the mirror, until he could tell the story... *at home*. When it was time to tell the story to the group, he froze up and had to resort to his notes. But it was clear that he *could* do it. Now he only had to overcome his personal fears. He was so despondent that he wondered whether he could even be a Waldorf teacher (He had taught in public schools before). I suggested he tell the story in front of children and not to worry about forgetting certain parts. And if he had to resort to the notes, so be it. It proved successful. The attentiveness of the children, their joy and anticipation drew the story out of him, making him feel more relaxed. He went on to become a successful class teacher.

The Waldorf student receives an immense treasure trove of stories over the course of twelve years. Scheherazade had to tell over a thousand stories lasting about three years before they *transformed* the king. The Waldorf student gets twelve years. After that they can *transform* the world, and they do. Like Malika Oufkir, all Waldorf teachers take on the task of Scheherazade.

---

[90] Padraic Colum, "Introduction," *The Complete Grimm's Fairy Tales* (New York: Pantheon Books, 1972) p. vii

[91] Chinua Achebe, *The Education of a British-Protected Child: Essays* (New York: Alfred A. Knopf, 2009).

[92] Malika Oufkir and Michéle Fitoussi (translated by Ros Schwartz), *Stolen Lives: Twenty Years in a Desert Jail* (New York: Miramax Books: Hyperion, 2000), p. 155.

[93] Ibid. p. 157.

The Eight-Year Journey

"I have never known a stupid educational program; they are always very clever. But what is important is that you have people in the school who can work in the way I have indicated."[94] ~ Rudolf Steiner

ANOTHER DISTINCTIVE element of Waldorf Schools is the ideal of having one teacher take a class through from first grade to eighth grade – the class teacher. A deepening relationship is built up between the children and their teacher over the years, one that is based on trust and love, and where the children feel seen by their teacher in who they really are as developing human beings. Thereby school becomes a second home for them, filled with the glowing atmosphere of warmth, happiness, and acceptance. That is the ideal.

A few years ago, our school was thinking of terminating the eight-year journey of the class teacher in favor of having middle grades teachers take over after fifth grade. Questions had arisen whether one teacher can really carry the eight-year load professionally, especially in the middle school when the academic pressures becomes more acute. Other questions included: do the students grow tired of their teacher? Can the teacher meet the changing needs of the student? Are the class teachers flexible enough to change with the students? What if there are problems with the respective teacher that do not get sufficiently addressed, are simply ignored, or allowed to continue? Does the class teacher rule his or her realm at the expense of the whole school? Are they too much like autonomous kings and queens, keeping special subject teachers at bay, making it more difficult for them to teach? Are too many students lost because of inadequate and underperforming class teachers? Is there a need for specialists?

We had, unfortunately, experienced some crises with teachers over the years, based on some of the above issues. Furthermore, our track record of having one class teacher go through the complete 8-year cycle was not very good, though there were legitimate reasons, such as maternity leave, having to move because of the partner, falling terminally ill, or otherwise indisposed.

These questions and arguments have been circulating for years, which has led to the shortening of the 8-year loop in a number of Waldorf Schools, even going so far as to divide the eight years into three sections. These queries have not only come from the outside but also from within the schools, parents and teachers alike. People lament that the students are not sufficiently met in the sciences and that there is a need for specially trained middle school teachers who can cope with the "academic rigors" demanded during these years. The need for rigor of content and new material, on the other hand, is rarely mentioned.

We decided to take up an all-faculty study, looking at the pros and cons of the eight-year loop. A number of parents who had voiced concerns or were interested in the issue were also invited. This study was scheduled to last a few weeks after which the Council of Teachers (the College) would decide whether to revert to a new looping format. I was asked to research the topic and introduce the study. Each week, after my short introduction, the faculty divided into various groups to discuss selected topics, ensuring that all voices would be heard. It was a fruitful endeavor and made all of us more aware of the strengths and weaknesses of the 8-year cycle. This study happened a couple of years before Waldorf 100, and served as an initial step for us as a school to go back to the source, examine Steiner's indications and how they have continued to be implemented and worked with in Waldorf schools throughout the world. At the completion of the study the school decided to stay with the eight-year cycle, though each year the fifth-grade class teacher would be given the option of returning to first grade or undergo a review process. Moreover, we would readily accept teachers who only wanted to teach the early grades. For the most part we had already been adhering to these guidelines, though they had not become policy. However, throughout our entire endeavor to understand the 8-year cycle, we were, in essence, circumventing the real and underlying question: *What does it mean to be a class teacher?* That is the fundamental question, especially now that we have stepped into the second century of Waldorf education, which demands a renewed and updated grasp of the initial ideals. In essence, the question addresses the responsibilities of the Main Lesson teacher.

All relationships are based on trust, love, and mutual recognition. And this is especially true for teachers and their relationships with their students. In the lower school this element of trust rests predominantly with the class teacher, as underscored by Francis Edmunds: "It applies particularly to the main lesson period with which the day begins [...]. It is here where the class teacher's role is paramount."[95] It takes time to get to know one another, and people also change over time, especially children. They grow and develop in leaps and bounds. Having had the privilege of taking a class through the eight-year cycle I can attest to how important it is to get to know the whole developing human being in order to find out how best to educate and to draw out the finest in each one of them. And that takes time. The very concept of the eight-year cycle is an element that drew me to Waldorf education, though I recognized some of the difficulties all too well. Steiner brought up the eight-year cycle repeatedly, right from the first day of his preparatory lectures and seminars to the first teachers of the Stuttgart Waldorf School. He ends *Discussion One* on September 21, 1919 with the words, "The teacher goes up the school with his class. The teacher of the highest class (Class VIII) then begins again with the lowest (Class 1)."[96]

If love is the foundation of Waldorf education, as Steiner repeatedly says in different ways, then we need to pursue those elements in education that support and cultivate that selfless love. My wife often brings up her class teacher, referring to the mood she conveyed, her humor, her rigor in both the academics and the arts – that she always had their backs, that she felt seen by her. Her trust in her class teacher was unequivocal, and when Fräulein Südow fell ill and the class had to have a substitute teacher, she missed her dearly, even the way she smelled (the Weleda creams) and dressed. She epitomized the ideal of the 8-year cycle.

As human beings we make mistakes, we say the wrong things, and we misinterpret situations. In fact, it is one of the reasons why teachers are called upon to look back over the day in the nightly *Rückschau*, which gives us the opportunity to become conscious of our deeds: what we need to work on and how we can do better next time. During this nightly practice where we try to glean the students' needs, we are supporting their growth. It helps us to see the child more fully – a crucial aspect of education, an education that does take time – a slow education. We are investing in a relationship with each individual child and the spirit of the class. It is our responsibility to tend that garden. We are building trust, mutual trust. Once that has been established and we know the children's strengths and weaknesses (how much they have progressed and improved, where they still need support), then we are beginning to teach "between the lines," between the rows or garden beds. We are taking the invisible into account, the nuances and subtleties that others, who do not know the children so well, might miss. Changing teachers every year would make that impossible. Our teaching becomes increasingly intuitive in regard to our handling of the class and the individual students. As we gently draw them out of themselves, they draw something out of us; they 'educate' us. It goes both ways – this deep knowing that develops over time. Steiner referred to this in various places as "spiritual fluidity."

We have to take into account the child's past, present, and future. Only then can we claim to educate the child for life (or lifetimes). It's what is often referred to as "the long haul." In that sense one can see these eight years as a *unity*, as a whole. And the eight years are like a *Gesamtkunstwerk*, as Caroline von Heidebrand wrote in her book, in which she outlined the first Waldorf curriculum. I like to think of it in terms of an octave: starting in first grade and slowly moving up until we again reach the same note, an octave up – transformed. The word cycle comes from the Greek *kuklos*, which means circle. The circle of this cycle has been completed. I carried that feeling of the 8 years as one whole within me right from first grade. It makes a profound difference if one teaches out of that idea (ideal) or not. Had I not been able to teach beyond that first year, it would still have made a difference, because inwardly I was holding all eight years. When I told the fairytales, I was building their vocabulary that they would need in the upper grades. When I mentioned the lion, I was already thinking of the fourth-grade block on animals; when introducing the numbers, I was knowingly thinking of fractions; during form drawing I anticipated the geometry block, which, in turn, would foreshadow algebra. The future, their future, lived within me. It was almost as if the future was leaning in and touching me and the children, as if it was approaching us, guiding us in some mysterious way. In an article that Erika Dühnfort wrote about the Waldorf class teacher for the "Erziehungskunst," she sums it up perfectly in the sentence:

"The class teacher must learn to bake tomorrow's bread today for the students."[97]

In *Practical Advice to Teachers*, Steiner alludes to the importance of introducing a topic in one year and then bringing it up many years later with greater understanding, which underscores the importance of a class teacher staying with her class as long as possible. He first talks about how Waldorf teachers must recognize life more profoundly if they want to educate the developing human being (knowledge that might have been secret in ancient mystery centers, knowledge that could not be conveyed directly). He takes this thought and leads it directly to why it is important for the class teacher to remain with his or her class.

> In a certain sense, all teachers must be in possession of truths that they cannot directly pass on to the world. [...] They [the students] will understand these teachings later, when you come back to them again and are then able to explain not only what you now tell them but also what they took in earlier.[98]

And directly after that he states:

> This works very strongly on the heart forces. That is why it is essential in any good school that the teacher remain with a single group of students for as long as possible. The teacher takes them the first year, continues with them the following year, moves again with them to the third year, and so on – as far as external circumstances will allow. And the teacher who has had the eighth grade one year should start again with the first grade the following year. It is sometimes appropriate to return only years later to something you have instilled into the children's souls. Whatever the circumstances, the education of the heart forces suffers if the children have a new teacher every year who cannot follow up what has

been instilled into their souls in previous years. It is a feature of this teaching method that the teacher moves up through the grades with the same students. Only in this way can one work with the rhythms of life. And life has a rhythm in the most comprehensive sense.[99]

In this regard, Rudolf Steiner, while lecturing in Torquay in 1924, England, spoke just as emphatically about the class teacher staying with his or her class:

Let me therefore give you an example of something that can sink into the child's soul so that it grows as the child grows, something that you can come back to in later years and use to arouse certain feelings. Nothing is more useful and fruitful in teaching than to give the children something in picture form between the seventh and eighth years, and later, perhaps in the fourteenth or fifteenth years, to come back to it again in some way or other. Just for this reason we try to let the children in the Waldorf School remain as long as possible with one teacher. When they come to school at seven years of age the children are given over to a teacher who then takes the class as far as possible, for it is good that things that at one time were given to the children in germ can again and again furnish the content of the methods used in their education.[100]

If asked, teachers will attest that this continuity over many years is somewhat like an inscrutable guiding hand, which can be felt in a palpable, almost tangible manner. It can also be observed from the outside and has long term effects. On one of our senior class trips, the second-grade teacher accompanied his former class to Italy. The seniors had vehemently lobbied for his presence on the trip and raised funds for him to be able to come. That's how much they loved him. When we came to Assisi, he and his former students experienced one of these "full-circle" moments when we walked through that medieval town, went to the cathedral, saw the Saint's robes, and went down to his tomb. It was truly moving to see and then to hear in our evening review how the students responded, remembering back to 2nd grade and their Saint Francis play. This teacher had also brought little notes from his current class to put into the grating of St. Francis's tomb, and he was given a whole bunch of cards as a gift for his second-grade students from one of the monks stationed at the tomb, on which was written the famous "Peace Prayer," beginning with the lines, "Lord, make me an instrument of your peace. Where there is hatred, let me sow love." Incredibly, the monk had randomly handed the teacher the exact number of cards needed for every child in his class. Fondly, the seniors remembered how they themselves used to recite the verse as little second graders.

Waldorf teachers are in it for the "long haul." And what a blessing it is to observe the children grow from the time their teeth are changing through to puberty and adolescence. It is a journey from the dreamy paradisal state through the imaginative feeling realm to the threshold of clear understanding. The call from the future will be stronger if we can hold the 8 years as a sacred unity. To break it up by consciously changing teachers in fifth or sixth grade will weaken this potential, especially if it is not necessary. Yes, we might still carry the whole, but if we know that we will not teach them beyond fifth grade, that we will not be teaching them physics, chemistry, or physiology, let alone world history in eighth grade, it will affect, in one way or another, the manner of our teaching. And that should not be underestimated. It was not for nothing that Steiner wanted the class teacher to accompany the children *for as long as possible*. The teaching will gain in breadth and depth. It allows a force, an imponderable force to enter the present moment. It helps to enflame, enthuse, enliven the present

moment – encouraging the child. What is important in this
8-year cycle is the journey from one phase to another. Had it
been possible to delay enrollment for a year, Steiner might
have decided on a seven-year loop. The 8-year cycle ensures
that the class teacher can be with the children for the entire
7-year phase of child development.

When the child enters first grade when it is six or seven
years old it leaves early childhood behind. The forces that
helped to build up the body and its internal organs are now
set free, and become active in the soul as memory and
intelligence. This birth of the life forces can now be utilized
for learning. During this second phase the child lives in the
rhythmic system. The child becomes an artist, wanting to
mold, paint, and draw. Just like the life forces built up the
bodily organs in the first seven-year cycle, now the freed life
forces want to form the world outwardly through art.
(*Kingdom of Childhood,* lecture 6). Through art and artistic
teaching (in contrast to instructions and imparting
techniques) we nurture the feeling life through pictorial
teaching that strengthens the will. The *astral body*
(encompassing soul capacities), though present, does not
come to full activity until around the 14th year, where it is
truly born, just like the etheric is born around the changing
of the teeth. But during the second seven-year cycle it is
gradually drawn inward, incarnating in the developing child
until it permeates it more fully.[101] In eighth grade, around
the 14th year, it passes through the threshold of puberty into
adolescence, inaugurating a very different consciousness.
With some children this shows itself very clearly already in
earlier years, and we can be misled into thinking they are
already fully mature, but inwardly they are still young and
need the clear guiding hand of the knowing and sensitive
class teacher. Likewise, some students are precocious and
extremely bright. As long as they have a wise and loving
teacher, offering abundant content and activities that appeal
to all the faculties of the child, the child will never be bored,
but feel connected to the greater world through the heart. In

the words of Francis Edmunds, "A deeper, richer life of heart is needed to humanize the intellect."[102] And especially in our abstract, technocratic, and intellectual times we need people who have the will power and the heart forces to bring positive change to the world. The pictorial image still remains the main medium, not the naked idea, the concept.

The eight years encompass and frame the second seven-year cycle, a time when the child needs and yearns for a strong figure of *authority*, an authority based on love and respect. During this developmental phase the child learns primarily through the imagination – content that is imbued with living pictures: moral imaginations. During this second phase the child is also learning healthy habits. Laying this foundation is best served through one teacher, one figure of loving authority, teaching artistically, thereby paving the way for high school where the intellect can prosper. Through teaching the content imaginatively the lower school prepares the path for critical thinking, which is based on the pursuit and nurturing of truth. From goodness (first 7 years) to beauty (second 7 years), to truth (third 7 years). To iterate: healthy habits take time, as does the cultivation of a worked through sense of beauty. Having time to guide students in these realms is a privilege; seeing them gradually improve, gain strength, and acquire skills is satisfying to all involved. During this second phase the children experience their soul life in the circulation of their blood and breath. And music helps to bind the etheric to the physical.

Right at the outset of her book on the Waldorf curriculum, Caroline von Heidebrand writes eloquently on the importance and relevancy of the 8-year cycle, reinforcing what has already been clearly stated: how the class teacher is able to have an overview of the entire curriculum and the great variety of subjects and how the children fare in them.[103] The educational practices, based in reality, then become "love deeds," (*Liebestaten*). Thus the class teacher, over a period of 8 years, gives a grand overview of the world, through the sciences and humanities and through the portal of the heart intelligence, which is the foundation for the awakening *astral* during adolescence (not to be confused with puberty, which leads up to *true* adolescence as it manifests itself in high school).

In this regard, we need to lay the groundwork so that the soul forces can flourish freely and not lag behind, which can easily occur in our intellectual age. Class teachers are quasi midwives during this second phase of child development, readying the students for the birth of the astral body, which then leads them into adolescence and the full brilliance of the intellect. Simultaneously they help the child to overcome the forces of inheritance.

As Steiner restated many times, both to the teachers and to the anthroposophists: the times, as bad as they are, will get increasingly worse in the future, which makes Waldorf education even more acute (underscored by the Covid 19 pandemic through which we are all suffering in one way or another, and which have thrown light on social inequities). We need to plant the seeds of self-education even more ardently, which means that much will depend on who we are as teachers, and what kind of role models we can be – must be – for the children. The class teacher becomes the foremost representative of the adult world. The way we work on ourselves will convey itself on the children, which, in turn, animates their desire to work on their own growth. And we should remember that the imitative forces are still incredibly strong in the young children of the lower grades. In the high school they need a teacher who embodies the highest ideals, who can guide them along like a mentor, a loyal older friend. Simply buddying up to the students will only have short term results.

Any art takes a long time to perfect. Think of how many years it takes to play an instrument skillfully, or to become proficient in drawing, sculpture, dancing, or any other artistic discipline. Steiner wanted the teachers to become artists, and that – as mentioned – takes time. The Teacher Education Institutes get the aspiring teachers started and introduce them to helpful approaches and techniques, show them what lies ahead, even send them into the classroom for observations and practicums, but that alone will never suffice. The substantial art of teaching is only learned in the classroom, together with the students who the teacher is responsible for, and with ardent study and practice at home, supported by an experienced mentor, and hopefully a musician or artist.

Entering a first grade and knowing that you will be together for a number of years – even if it is not all eight years – makes a huge difference in attitude. It's like a cushion of air that surrounds the teacher and the children. *We are on this journey together.* And as Waldorf teachers we know that the knowledge that we have to impart is only one, though significant aspect. More important is how they'll fare in life once they leave school; to what extent their will forces have been strengthened in order for them to be resilient and self-reliant people. Will they have the strengths to do what is expected of them, what they expect of themselves? That will, in part, depend on the capacities they acquired during their time in school. Moreover, *how* will they view life as such? For instance, has their sense of beauty been sufficiently developed so that they can bring beauty – inner and outer – to the world? Beauty has been undermined in conventional education, considered unessential. Modernity has lost the sense of beautification's importance in the world – how it changes, uplifts, strengthens, and inspires people. Furthermore, authentic beauty is tantamount to a moral force within a person, which will initiate meaningful actions that will help, heal, and enhance people. Too much in the world causes pain, makes life more difficult, and puts hurdles in the way of progress.

There is an endearing story told by René Maikowski, (who was asked by Rudolf Steiner to teach in the pioneering Waldorf School in Essen, Germany), which highlights the deep and intuitive relationship between the children and their class teacher. It was, as he recounts, a time of great collegial conflict in the school, and the situation got so dire that Maikowski, after a particularly difficult College meeting, decided to leave the school. The very next morning during Main Lesson, a boy in his fifth-grade class suddenly stood up and said, "Mr. Maikowski, last night I dreamed that you were leaving the school. If you do that, I am going to cry so much that the whole school is going to be under water." The rest of the class immediately chimed in, pleading with him to stay. René Maikowski, who had not told a soul about his decision, was so astonished at this spontaneous outburst that he promised to stay with them through to eighth grade (after which he left).[104] There's more to the relationship between the students and their teacher than one might think.

Nurturing a sense of truth also takes time. Goodness, beauty, and truth are at the core of Waldorf education, and their foundation is to be laid in the early years of the child's education, and the class teacher holds tremendous responsibility in this regard. Giving them eight years to build on those lofty ideals is a pedagogical boon that is not found in any other educational system to that degree.

On September 3, 1924 Rudolf Steiner voiced his intention of giving a lecture cycle on the moral foundations of Waldorf education at the end of the month or in the first week of October. Those were the last words that he spoke to the teachers in Stuttgart. Unfortunately, his failing health prevented him from giving this course.[105] Ernst Weissert, in an article commemorating the 50th anniversary of the Stuttgart Waldorf School wrote that shortly beforehand, Steiner mentioned how education needs to turn toward the arts 180 degrees (my loose translation).[106] The arts are a powerful tool for self-transformation and infuse an understanding of any subject with beauty, meaning and life. We need to learn how to teach as artistically as possible to fire up the students' enthusiasm for learning.

The country schools in Germany (Dorfschulen) also went up to 8th grade. In many ways they were like the one-room-schoolhouse that we could find all over America. Just down the road from us we have a building near to our Waldorf school that used to be a one-room-school building (a notion I rather like: the idea of education having flourished in our "happy valley" long before the Waldorf School started). But the class teacher is something utterly different to what these early country teachers were like. Instead of taking one class through the eight years, they taught all age groups in one room. The old system was based on learning by rote and was very strict and limited. (Laura Ingalls Wilder gives a vivid and heartfelt account of the teaching style of the one-room-schoolhouse in the late 1800's in her *Little House on the Prairie* Series.)

Questions about the 8-year cycle of Waldorf Schools have existed for decades, and every school should regularly review how it is faring in this regard. How do we stand with the eight-year cycle, both as a school and as a movement? In many of the schools where the looping has been reduced, the class teachers are not necessarily happy about the restrictions, even the ones who have consciously opted to teach a limited cycle. Dividing up the eight years between different class teachers adds to the widespread fragmentation that already exists in our current society. It was prevalent in Steiner's time as well, but to a lesser extent. It goes hand in hand with the fragmentation of the schedule, where schools choose to extend the day, shorten the recess time, and add more classes. Our fast-paced age needs the opposite. The fact that the children enter the schools with a great variety of "disabilities," struggle with ADHD, speech defects, traumatic home situations, while inundated with electronic media, calls for greater calm, less deadening intellectuality, more time to "play," and ample time to truly immerse in one topic over a longer period of time – which was the initial idea of the Main Lesson. The class teacher is the remedy to erosive fragmentation.

Children deserve the best, and anybody who takes education seriously knows and feels that there is a component to teaching that is *sacred.* It is a sacred art, because life is sacred, made most visible in the growing children. When the move is made toward breaking up the unity of the 8-year cycle, we are forfeiting the "sacred art" and the sacredness of the second seven-year cycle. Or forgetting it. We've lost trust in the wisdom of the sacred, arguing eloquently why we need to have a mini high school before high school. What is often overlooked is that after the Main Lesson the learners are anyway taught by specialists, which creates a fructifying balance between the specialist and the class teacher, especially if there is a culture of teachers working together in collegial harmony, which can be achieved in faculty meetings or discussions between teachers over coffee in the faculty room.

All teachers need to remain fresh, vibrant, enthusiastic, and engaged. And what better way to achieve that than through new material every year, as already mentioned earlier in the book. Generally, the new material excites the class teachers. Yes, I did get anxious, and there were elements that I experienced as a burden, but my enthusiasm was sparked at the idea of learning something new that I could then impart to the students. It's what puts spring and élan into the teachers' footsteps. It's a natural human trait that when we get animated by something, we want to share our knowledge, talk about it, and let others know. Delving into new disciplines stimulates our minds and imaginations, keeps us young, and makes us into Renaissance people. And what better example for the students than to see a person able to do and be interested in so many divergent disciplines – always trying, always attempting something new and different, always striving to do one's best. And failing in between, but finding solutions, resolving problems, moving on. The extra effort that the teacher has to invest will, in turn, be taken up by the students to a much greater degree than if the content had not been a challenge to the teacher. That very effort helps to prevent teachers from getting sour, bored, and drained. Our age is so specialized, and for the children to experience a teacher who tackles every subject

– and often in an uncanny knowledgeable manner that even impress the experts – is a gift that is worth far more than actually getting a slew of experts in, who might not be as excited, who might not be able to impart the knowledge in such an animated way, or who might never have struggled as much to attain their knowledge. In this regard Steiner's words, also from lecture 4 in the *Kingdom of Childhood*, can offer comfort:

> For you see, whenever you undertake a spiritual activity, you always must be able to bear being clumsy and awkward. People who cannot endure being clumsy and doing things stupidly and imperfectly at first never really will be able to do them perfectly in the end out of their own inner self. And especially in education first of all you must kindle in your own souls what you then have to work out for yourselves; but first it must be enkindled in your soul. If once or twice you have succeeded in thinking out a pictorial presentation of a lesson that you see impresses the children, then you will make a remarkable discovery about yourself. You will see that it becomes easier to invent such pictures, that by degrees you become inventive in a way you had never dreamed of. But for this you must have the courage to be very far from perfect to begin with.[107]

To *"have the courage to be very far from perfect to begin with."* What a statement! It is a comforting sort of valor to pursue. This is especially true for class teachers who are confronted with subjects that they are not so familiar with, or that demand skills they lack or have to work on. Statements like the one above gives one hope that, "Yes, I can succeed if I persevere." It animates the Scheherazade within us. In a similar vein Steiner states in *Balance in Teaching*:

> You would have taught best of all if each morning you had gone into your class in fear and trembling, without very much confidence in yourself. [...] [I]t depends

upon your constantly having had the feeling that you are growing while you are helping the children to grow, the feeling that you are experimenting in the highest sense of the word, that you are not really able to do so very much, but working with the children there grows in you a certain strong capacity.[108]

A class teacher who has to grapple with a subject, might find the right way of conveying the information and content, because of the very fact that they have to struggle through the steps themselves. That certainly happened to me. I was fearful of teaching the sciences, but once I entered into the topic and understood the fundamentals, I was more than eager to do the experiments with the students, feeling like a magician with my test tubes and Bunsen burners. Steiner saw no need for specialists in the lower school or in the middle school, because the learners are still within the second seven-year cycle.

Perhaps you will say you ought never to be a teacher if you have to appear before the children in this awkward manner. But here indeed the anthroposophical outlook must help you along. You must say to yourself: Something is leading me karmically to the children so that I can be with them as a teacher though I am still awkward and clumsy. And those before whom it behooves me not to appear clumsy and awkward – those children – I shall only meet in later years, again through the workings of karma.[109]

In the third seven-year cycle during high school we have the specialists who won't appear clumsy and awkward. The students now also expect the teachers to be experts in their fields.

Steiner wanted the teachers to be and feel as *free* as possible to work with the material in their own individual ways. We have to remember, as Waldorf teachers it is not a matter of intellectual prowess, it's about educating the whole human being and getting the students to a place where they are excited about learning. Having acquired the skills and confidence they now feel equipped to meet the world and forge their own way ahead, knowing that they are able to do whatever they set their minds to – just like their class teacher did for them over eight years.

When the seventh grader studies the Renaissance, what better way than to be taught by a Renaissance person – not a specialist – a person who has the pluck and ability to tackle and grapple with every subject, and convey it in the most artistic way possible. A class teacher needs to develop into a true Renaissance person, and by the time they have arrived at the seventh grade they will already have covered a very impressive academic terrain. The teacher can refer to almost every subject and make connections, because they have taught every subject.

Look at Raphael's *School of Athens*: all these great innovators, these initiates, who are depicted discussing, conversing and debating with one another about the broadest and biggest questions of life; observe with what dedication, for instance, Euclid is teaching his little group of students on the lower right hand side, how reverently and intently they are focused on their beloved teacher's actions, how the one student is lovingly touching the shoulder of his fellow student: to me it epitomizes the Waldorf mood. That is the Renaissance spirit that connects the stars to the earth, links thinking with the physical world. Plato points up to the divine world – a reminder from where humanity has come – and Aristotle's hand faces downward toward the temporal world: a beautiful and wisdom filled rendering of heaven and earth. And it is these very diverse connections that the class teacher can make that a specialist might not be able to weave in so effortlessly.

In the lower school the children need to be strengthened in every area. And they find comfort and confidence by the rhythms that run throughout each lesson, day, and year, until the completion of the eight-year cycle. They can rest and rely on the known rhythms, which serve not only as a strong foundation, but allow for sturdy walls to be built around them, and a roof over their heads. School becomes the house of learning – a home for the soul to flourish in.

Ideally speaking, they know that the world can be a good and beautiful place. Let's not expose and shock them too soon by all the monstrous things going on in the world, the atrocities we find in history. Young children need protection. That does not mean we smother them. Our long-term aim is that we strengthen them so that they can go out into the unknow to meet and transform the ugly elements of the world, but they can be woken up gradually, gently. Parzival could only achieve what he did because he grew up in the seclusion of Soltane, a nature boy, who could do as he pleased in his own paradise until he was ready to go into the unknown. He was given the time to play and learn at his own pace. The same was true for Buddha. He was secluded and shielded from death, poverty, ugliness, old age, and suffering, till the time was ripe. Timing plays an essential role in life. Bringing content to the students at the right time is a source of healing. Age appropriate teaching is healing teaching. When we supply them with surroundings that they can trust, know, and discover to be beautiful and good, then we prepare them to meet the truths of the greater world, no matter how ugly. They will have the capacities and resilience to do something about it, to go out into the world and make a difference. And that is exactly what many of them do.

The class teacher is an important "known" in this education: a person whose hand they shake every day, who they trust, and who loves them and cares for them, long after they have left school. It is always a pleasure to catch up with former students, to talk to them, find out what they are doing, what they have done – and reflect on their schooling, what worked, what didn't. In many cases the class teacher replaces the parent as the person who translates the world for them. Steiner recommended that, if possible, the child would do best by being at home for the first seven years, the second phase to have one teacher who represents the world for them, and in the high school to have many teachers who teach them how to think, to form judgements, and to deepen their understanding of cause and effect.

And they especially need teachers who can see them through times of crises. Merely entering the school is a form of crisis for many children, coinciding with the change of teeth. It certainly was for me (though I did not have the good fortune of a Waldorf school). It is part of the lawfulness of growing up. The theme of "death and rebirth," which Goethe followed consciously in his own life, runs through the rhythms of all of our lives. In that sense the human being is born repeatedly, each birth preceded by a little death, a growth crisis, each one leading us a step closer to ourselves, our destiny. We as teachers know about them, we prepare for them (though they can still take us by surprise by their vehemence).

The next major crisis comes in the form of the 9-year change, which is as significant as the 12-year change, which is the third crisis. The class teacher will know whether his class is ahead or behind, developmentally, and can act and teach accordingly – which would not happen as easily otherwise. The middle school children need the continuity of the class teacher even more – that one person who can understand them, as they go through the stages of puberty (not yet true adolescence). During the year 12 crisis they go through enough divisiveness without also having to bear the loss of their beloved class teacher.

It is helpful to remember that each phase brings with it a change of consciousness, and the class teacher has the humbling privilege of facilitating all three of these major changes: change of teeth, nine-year change, 12-year change, and then handing them over when true adolescence begins (when both physical and psychological maturity merge) – the fourth major crisis. Rudolf Steiner addresses these pivotal points in lecture eleven of *The Foundations of Human*

Experience, when he urges the teachers to observe the students carefully, how they look in regard to their growth; between growing too "lanky" with too much emphasis on memory, or too "stocky" with too much emphasis on the imagination. The ideal is to find a balance between the two.

> That is why it is so important that you have the same children during all of the school years, and why it is so idiotic that children have a different teacher every year. However, there is another side to this. At the beginning of each school year and at the beginning of each developmental period (at seven, nine, and twelve years of age), teachers slowly come to know the children. They come to know children who are clearly the imagination type who recognize everything, and they come to know children who are clearly memory types who can remember everything. Teachers must also become familiar with this.[110]

Only in high school can we observe the birth of authentic critical thinking skills, though there too it is still in its infancy (not the way it "should be," according to abstract notions, but the way it is). By fourteen the thinking is still strongly colored by feelings, and it takes some time before it becomes detached and can stand on its own free-thinking-feet with confidence. Teaching students how to think logically and clearly, based on a sense of truth, runs throughout the high school, stepwise. By fourteen the analytical and critical thinking faculty begins to emerge. Much like the consciousness of the 9th grader, it remains an ongoing challenge for many people in our time, when judgements are made all too rashly, without thinking things through to the last degree. People routinely form uninformed opinions, taking sides on issues, where everything is either black or white, right or wrong, where subtleties are lost, and where the feelings easily cloud judgements. However, it is what makes high school teaching so exciting – the pursuit of truth through clear and living thinking. The arts and crafts strongly support this. The lawfulness of the physical that needs to be followed in making a dovetail box, or the detailed observational drawing of a still life, lead to a truthful, corrective relationship to the world. While many students still have difficulties navigating their own thought life, interestingly enough they are highly conscious and perceptive when it comes to muddy thinking on the part of the teachers. Nevertheless, with the right questions and pictures the most inspiring thoughts arise, where one can get the sense of past lives shining through.

Werner Glas, on writing about the significant connections the class teacher achieves over a period of eight years, sums it up succinctly in four main points:

1. It enables the teacher to develop a continuous and deepening knowledge of his [and her] children.
2. It brings about an increasingly intimate connection between teacher and parents.
3. It gives the teacher a wider horizon and greater challenge. The teacher who faces a new situation each year and who has to adapt both new materials and new stages of maturity in his [and her] pupils must remain inwardly creative, and [her] professional work helps [her] as a growing individuality.
4. The interrelationship between subject matter taught in earlier and later years adds unique possibilities to his task. [S]He knows what the children have experienced, [s]he can allow a theme to be forgotten and reawakened in another form at a later date, and [s]he can throw many bridges between disciplines, which are usually separated academically. In this way [s]he works toward the unification of experience and a sense of relatedness in knowledge, with

the image of [the human being] as its coordinating point.[111]

There is no perfect Waldorf school, or perfect curriculum, or perfect anything. But there is the striving toward maximizing the pedagogical potential, and to uphold that which holds true to our age, the "Consciousness Soul Age," which will still last for a while. It began in 1413 and will end in 3573. Keeping that in mind, without going into any depth or breadth, it means that the enduring hallmarks of Waldorf education will not only stand the test of time and remain relevant, but become ever more needed and important as the challenges toward a healthy, uplifting culture will increase.

The ideal is having kindergarten through 12th grade in one school. There is a natural transition between early childhood and the grades, and then another natural transition between the grades and high school. All three relate to the different phases. If we consciously decide to treat the middle school as a completely separate entity, then we are breaking up the second seven-year cycle, which Steiner always saw as a unity, even though there is a clear development within that second cycle. Furthermore, if the children do not receive one class teacher who will teach all the remaining Main Lessons, but only a few, then it will be not much different from the high school experience. A "homeroom" teacher will not be able to replace the depth of relatedness between the student and the class teacher. We consequently weaken and lessen the impact of the break between the grades and the high school. We must remember that the analytical, critical faculty is only freed around the age of fourteen, no matter how precocious and mature some students might seem. The apparent intellectual and physical prematurity often comes at the expense of soul capacities, causing an arrested soul development that can go into the twenties and even beyond.

If we hold true to the freedom of the class teacher, then the class teacher should also have the freedom to continue if she feels and knows she can, and if it is recognized by the faculty. Conversely, the class teacher might also know that he can only carry a class responsibly for a shorter number of years. And likewise, it is prudent to review a class and their teacher every few years, since there are always situations and circumstances that make it evident that a class teacher should not continue with a class. All the questions brought at the beginning of this chapter are legitimate. There are some inherent problems with the 8-year cycle. Taking on a class for eight years is not for everyone. It is a huge commitment, and it should not be held against those who choose to teach a shorter loop. Over the years we have had teachers who have requested team teaching. One of our sons had two class teachers while we lived in Switzerland for a year. They shared the blocks between them. And in some cases, it is not a matter of ability or competency in the material, but of the teacher not wanting to take on the responsibility for a class over so many years. The devotion to being a class teacher is not necessarily as strong as it used to be. Many teachers have outside interests that they want to pursue. This almost monastic devotion to being a class teacher is getting increasingly rare, especially compared to some of the pioneers of Waldorf education. For instance, Daniel Johan van Bemmelen and others of the founding teachers of the Den Haag Waldorf School in Holland, initially did not receive a salary, even paying for supplies out of pocket.[112] That kind of sacrifice would be rare today.

We need to brace ourselves against criticisms and know why we do what we do, based on experience. If we succumb to the intellectual pressures, the rushed education, then we become part of the system. Education needs to remain free and be part of the free spiritual life. It is in danger of losing that autonomy. There are enough constraints coming at the Waldorf movement from the outside, without our education being compromised from within the movement. The schools in Britain, Holland, and Canada, to name a few places, have to contend with numerous outside restrictions from their respective governments because they are government funded to a large degree. And here in America we see it fast encroaching. Do we challenge it, or do we succumb – even if we don't have to?

If we rely on specialists in the middle school, we run the risk of hurrying the thinking stage, not allowing the pictorial element to take full effect. And as Francis Edmunds said, "The transition from the pure fantasy [imagination] of the little child to the abstract thought of later years should be a gentle process."[113] It demands artistic rigor in the broadest and deepest sense of the word, so that we can draw forth clear thinking in the upper grades, so that the high school will truly be the crowning of the student's Waldorf education.

The world needs people who have been educated in their will, practiced in the arts, and have become highly skillful with their hands; people who are insightful, perceptive, and observant, and who can penetrate and navigate the abundance of lies and falsehoods of the modern world. *If* the second seven-year cycle is filled with harmonizing activities, practical experiences steeped in reality, imaginative rich story content of the most universal kind (which instills reverence and respect through a healthy social life in the classroom), and where every student can develop their unique gifts, *then a solid foundation has been poured.* All these capacities will strengthen, support, and lead to self-development right up into old age.

And what a privilege it is to be able to go through eight years with a highly respected class teacher and a group of fellow classmates, learning and doing the most diverse things, where they get to know each other so intimately, and accept each other's strengths and weaknesses. It is not always an easy road, but no road to freedom ever is. It certainly will not have been commonplace. The teacher and the students will have gone on a wonderful journey together, never to be forgotten. The students now feel ready to meet what high school has to offer with a fresh sense of independence. And as a teacher one has received a memorable lesson in humility and patience.

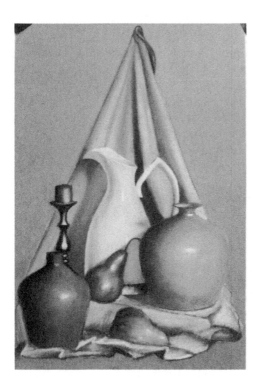

[94] Rudolf Steiner, *The Kingdom of Childhood* (Anthroposophic Press, 1995), p. 19.

[95] Francis Edmunds, *And Introduction to Waldorf Education* (Sophia Books, 2004), p. 35.

[96] Rudolf Steiner, *Discussion with Teachers* (London: Rudolf Steiner Press, 1967), p. 24.

[97] Erika Dühnfort, „Der Klassenlehrer," *Soziale Erneuerung als Ursprung und Ziel der Freien Waldorfschule: 50 Jahre Pädagogik Rudolf Steiners Festschrift der „Erziehungskunst"* (Stuttgart: Verlag Freies Geistesleben, 1969), p. 386.

[98] Rudolf Steiner, *Practical Advice to Teachers* (Anthroposophic Press, 2000), p. 84.

99 Ibid. pp. 84-85

100 Rudolf Steiner, *The Kingdom of Childhood* (Anthroposophic Press), 1995, p. 57.

101 Rudolf Steiner, *The Kingdom of Childhood* (Anthroposophic Press, 1995), Lecture 6.

102 L. Francis Edmunds, *Rudolf Steiner Education* (London: Rudolf Steiner Press, 1962).

103 Caroline von Heidebrand, *Der Lehrplan der Freien Waldorfschule* (Stuttgart: Freies Geistesleben, 1975), p. 13-15.

104 René Maikowski, *Schicksalswege auf der Suche nach dem lebendigen Geist* (Freiburg: Verlag Die Kommenden, 1980), p. 134

105 Rudolf Steiner delivered his last lecture on September 28, 1924.

106 *Soziale Erneuerung als Ursprung und Ziel der Freien Waldorfschule: 50 Jahre Pädagogik Rudolf Steiners Festschrift der „Erziehungskunst"* (Verlag Freies Geistesleben, 1969), p. 320.

107 Rudolf Steiner, *The Kingdom of Childhood* (Anthroposophic Press, 1995), Lecture 4, p. 56-57.

108 Rudolf Steiner, *Balance in Teaching* (Anthroposophic Press, 2007), p. 8.

109 109 Rudolf Steiner, *The Kingdom of Childhood* (Anthroposophic Press, 1995), p. 57.

110 Rudolf Steiner, *The Foundations of Human Experience* (Anthroposophic Press, 1996), p. 181.

111 Werner Glas, *Speech Education in the Primary Grades of Waldorf Schools* (Sunbridge College Press, 1974,) p. 11.

112 Frans Lutters, *Daniel van Bemmelen: Wiedergeboren am Beginn des Lichten Zeitalters*, (Verlag am Michaelshof, 2012).

113 Francis Edmunds, *An Introduction to Steiner Education* (Sophia Books, 2004), p. 40.

A Legacy of Love[114]
Waldorf 100

"Where is the book in which the teacher can read about what teaching is? The children themselves are the book."
~ Rudolf Steiner

WHAT IS MOST striking during this celebratory centennial is to observe the extent to which Waldorf education has been expanded and spread to the farthest corners of the world by some of the most unlikely people. In the span of a mere hundred years this movement has grown from a single seedling school in Stuttgart, Germany, with 252 students to one of the largest independent school movements in the world, numbering well over 1,000 schools and 2,000 kindergartens worldwide, educating tens of thousands of students.

Every anniversary can serve as a Janus moment, an opportunity to look back, take stock, and reflect on the achievements of Waldorf education, while simultaneously looking ahead to what the future might hold – how it can be met and shaped. Waldorf 100 allows us to celebrate and admire the astounding accomplishments of this unique education as well as urging us to recall and return to the source – to become more conscious of the inaugural impulses that have contributed to the undeniable success of the movement.

Right from its festive opening celebration on September 7, 1919, Waldorf education was built on the foundation of tremendous *idealism*. Waldorf 100 is a welcomed call to once again remind us of the founding principles, which from its inception has created such awe-inspiring results. A closer look at these initial impulses reveal enduring values, confirming why this education has grown so rapidly and was able to overcome the most trying and nigh insurmountable difficulties, breaking national, racial, political, gender, religious, and social boundaries to become an educational movement that has universal appeal.

It took tremendous *courage* and *hope* to open the school, standing, as it did, in strong contrast to the mainstream educational system. In Waldorf education, Steiner outlined an approach that would provide solutions to the great social travails of the time (just after World War I) and those to come. We forget how radical his ideas were at the time, and indeed, still are to this day, though they have taken on new dimensions and perspectives within the current cultural, economic, and socio-political framework. But they have taken root, and proven themselves many times over. In short, Waldorf education is a human-centered education based on love: love for learning, love for life, love for the world, and love for one's fellow human being. Love is the key to the essence of Waldorf education.

In that sense, it was first and foremost a social impulse. Steiner often stressed the importance of people meeting one another with *interest*, which is the foundation of love. For the teacher it means recognizing the needs of each child. In order to do that, Waldorf teachers must deepen their understanding of the human being, thereby developing the faculties to "read" what each child needs, appropriate to their age and as an individual. And one can only truly know the human being if one understands the world. This presupposes that teachers remain learners throughout their lives.

Another maxim of Waldorf education, underscored by Rudolf Steiner from the outset, is that it remains grounded in practical life. This is especially pertinent for our digital age, so dominated by the intellect at the cost of other human faculties. Teaching with imagination stirs the feeling life of the children, which in turn wants to be transformed into an activity – to embody what they have been taught. Consequently, they arrive more easily at a well-rounded understanding of the respective subject matter. In this way, the *whole* human being is involved: head, heart, and limbs. However, this only works if the education is steeped in the artistic. This artistic element, fueled by enthusiasm, helps to make education joyful. And if all the lessons are permeated with truth, beauty, and goodness, then the children will thrive.

Waldorf education is a seedling education, where everything that is taught has the possibility for further growth. What is forgotten does not necessarily lose its power to change, metamorphose, and supply nourishment in the future. In that sense, this education is truly an education for life.

At the 50th anniversary of Waldorf education in Stuttgart in 1969, Herbert Hahn said that what was true for the founding of the Waldorf School in 1919, would still hold true for the next fifty years. I am convinced that these core impulses will continue to maintain their enduring value for the next hundred years.

During this festive time, it behooves us to honor the people who have gone before us: the teachers, parents, students, and friends alike, who have contributed in some way to the success of the movement, especially Emil Molt and Rudolf Steiner, the earthly and spiritual founders of Waldorf education. But even as we celebrate, we have to continue to deepen our understanding of the world and humanity, to connect with the true and good spirit of our age, and so plant new kernels that can flourish throughout the course of the next hundred years.

Thus, in the words of Rudolf Steiner at the last address to the students in Stuttgart, on the 30th April, 1924, less than a year before his death:

"Onwards, my dear students and my dear teachers, onwards!"[115]

[114] This article first appeared in the Hawthorne Valley Newsletter, and in the Calendar, https://hawthornevalley.org/waldorf-100-a-legacy-of-love/

[115] Berthold Faig, „Grundsteinlegung – Grundsteinspruch." *Soziale Erneuerung als Ursprung und Ziel der Freien Waldorfschule: 50 Jahre Pädagogik Rudolf Steiners Festschrift der „Erziehungskunst"* (Stuttgart: Verlag Freies Geistesleben, 1969), p. 315 (Translated by the author).

Bibliography

Achebe, Chinua. *The Education of a British-Protected Child: Essays.* New York: Alfred A. Knopf, 2009.

Aeppli, Willi. *The Care and Development of the Human Senses.* Translated by Valerie Freilich, revised. Forest Row: Steiner Schools Fellowship Publications, 1993.

Blanning, Nancy. "Foreword." In *The Mood of the Fifth: A Musical Approach To Early Childhood*, edited by Nancy Foster. Spring Valley: WECAN, 2013.

Brass, Reinhild. „Schöpferisches Musizieren – Musik in der Widarschule." In *Erziehen und Heilen durch Musik,* Herausgegeben von Gerhard Beilharz. Stuttgart: Verlag Freies Geistesleben, 1989.

Colum, Padraic. "Introduction." In *The Complete Grimm's Fairy Tales.* New York: Pantheon Books, 1972.

Dühnfort, Erika. „Der Klassenlehrer," In *Soziale Erneuerung als Ursprung und Ziel der Freien Waldorfschule: 50 Jahre Pädagogik Rudolf Steiners Festschrift der „Erziehungskunst."* Schriftleitung, Doktor Helmut von Kügelgen, Stuttgart: Verlag Freies Geistesleben, 1969.

Edmunds, Francis. *An Introduction to Steiner Education: The Waldorf School.* Forest Row: Sophia Books, 2004.

Edmunds, Francis. *Rudolf Steiner Education: The Waldorf Impulse.* London: Rudolf Steiner Press, 1962.

Faig, Berthold. "Grundsteinlegung – Grundsteinspruch." *Soziale Erneuerung als Ursprung und Ziel der Freien Waldorfschule: 50 Jahre Pädagogik Rudolf Steiners Festschrift der „Erziehungskunst."* Stuttgart: Verlag Freies Geistesleben, 1960.

Finser, Torin M. *School as a Journey: The Eight-Year Odyssey of a Waldorf Teacher and his Class.* Anthroposophic Press, 1994.

Friedman, Thomas and MacKillop. *The Copy Book:*

Mastering Basic Grammar and Style. New York: Holt, Reinhart and Winston, 1980.

Glas, Werner. *Speech Education in the Primary Grades of Waldorf Schools*. Sunbridge College Press, 1974.

Glöckler, Michaela. *Truth, Beauty and Goodness: The Future of education, healing arts and health care*. Hudson, NY: Waldorf Publications, 2019.

Grosse, Rudolf. *Erlebte Pädagogik: Schicksal und Geistesweg*. Dornach: Verlag am Goetheanum, 1998.

Heidebrand, Caroline von. *Der Lehrplan der Freien Waldorfschule*. Stuttgart: Freies Geistesleben, 1975.

Hoerner, Wilhelm. *Kosmische Rhythmen im Menschenleben*. Stuttgart: Urachhaus, 1990.

Holdrege, Craig, ed. *The Dynamic Heart and Circulation*. Translation by Katherine Creeger. Fair Oaks: AWSNA, 2002.

Jonathan Jansen with Nangamso Koza and Lihlumelo Toyana. *Great South African Teachers: A tribute to South Africa's great teachers from the people whose lives they have changed*. Johannesburg: Bookstorm and Pan Macmillan, 2011.

Kornberger, Horst. *The Power of Stories: Nurturing Children's Imagination and Consciousness*. Floris Books, 2008.

Kranich, Ernst Michael. „Die Verbindung des Werdenden Menschen mit den Kräften des Moralischen." *In Moralische Erziehung: Beiträge zur Pädagogik Rudolf Steiners*. Herausgegeben von der Pädagogischen Forschungstelle beim Bund der Freien Waldorfschulen durch Ernst-Michael Kranich. Stuttgart: Verlag Freies Geistesleben, 1994.

Lutters, Frans. *Daniel van Bemmelen: Wiedergeboren am Beginn des Lichten Zeitalters*. Verlag am Michaelshof, 2012.

Maikowski, René. *Schicksalswege auf der Suche nach dem lebendigen Geist*. Freiburg: Verlag Die Kommenden, 1980.

Matthews, Paul. *Words in Place: Reconnecting with Nature Through Creative Writing.* Hawthorne Press, 2007.
Müller, Eric G. *Life Poems for My Students: Birthday and other Verses.* Alkion Press, 2016.
Müller, Heinz. *Healing Forces in the Word and its Rhythms: Report Verses in Rudolf Steiner's Art of Education.* Forest Row: Rudolf Steiner Schools Fellowship Publications, 1983.
Oufkir, Malika, and Michéle Fitoussi. *Stolen Lives: Twenty Years in a Desert Jail.* Translated by Ros Schwartz. New York: Miramax Books: Hyperion, 2000.
Slezak-Schindler, Christa. *Künstlerisches Sprechen im Schulalter: Grundlegendes für Lehrer und Erzieher.* Stuttgart: Pädagogische Forschungsstelle beim Bund der Freien Waldorf Schulen, 1978.
Steiner, Rudolf. *Discussion with Teachers.* Translated by Helen Fox. London: Rudolf Steiner Press, 1967.
Steiner, Rudolf. *Rudolf Steiner Konferenzen mit den Lehrern der Freien Waldorfschule in Stuttgart. Erste Band.* GA 300/1. Dornach: Rudolf Steiner Verlag, 1975.
Steiner, Rudolf. *Verses and Meditations.* Translated by George and Mary Adams. London: Rudolf Steiner Press, 1979.
Steiner, Rudolf. *The Inner Nature of Music and the Experience of Tone.* Translated by Maria St. Goar. Spring Valley, New York: The Anthroposophic Press, 1983.
Steiner, Rudolf. *Soul Economy and Waldorf Education.* Translated by Roland Everett. Spring Valley NY: Anthroposophic Press, 1986.
Steiner, Rudolf. *Speech and Drama.* Translated by Mary Adams. Spring Valley: Anthroposophic Press,1986.
Steiner Rudolf. *The Spirit of the Waldorf School: Lectures Surrounding the Founding of the First Waldorf School.* Translated by Robert F. Lathe and Nancy Parsons Whittaker. Anthroposophic Press, 1995.
Steiner, Rudolf. *Kingdom of Childhood.* Translation by

Helen Fox, revised. Anthroposophic Press, 1995.

Steiner, Rudolf. *The Child's Changing Consciousness: As the Basis of Pedagogical Practice.* Translated by Roland Everett, revised. Anthroposophic Press, 1996.

Steiner, Rudolf. *The Foundations of Human Experience.* Translated by Robert F. Lathe and Nancy Parsons Whittaker. Anthroposophic Press, 1996.

Steiner, Rudolf. "Social Basis for Public Education." Stuttgart, June 1, 1919. In *Education as a Force for Social Change.* Translated by Robert F. Lathe and Nancy Parsons Whittaker. Anthroposophic Press, 1997.

Rudolf Steiner, *Faculty Meetings with Rudolf Steiner: Volume 1.* Translated by Robert Lathe and Nancy Parsons Whittaker. Anthropsophic Press, 1998.

Steiner, Rudolf. *Faculty Meetings with Rudolf Steiner: Volume 2.* Translated by Robert Lathe and Nancy Parsons Whittaker. Anthroposophic Press, 1998.

Steiner, Rudolf. *Practical Advice to Teachers.* Translated by Johanna Collis. Anthroposophic Press, 2000.

Steiner, Rudolf. *Human Values in Education: The Foundations in Waldorf Education.* Translated by Vera Compton, revised. Anthroposophic Press, 2004.

Steiner, Rudolf. *Modern Art of Education.* Ilkley, 1923. Translated by Jesse Darrel. Anthroposophic Press, 2004.

Steiner, Rudolf. *The Essentials of Education.* London: Rudolf Steiner Press, 1968.

Steiner, Rudolf. *Balance in Teaching.* Translated by Ruth Pusch, revised. Anthroposophic Press, 2007.

Weißert, Ernst. „Von den Motiven und Lebensphasen der Schulbewegung." In *Soziale Erneuerung als Ursprung und Ziel der Freien Waldorfschule: 50 Jahre Pädagogik Rudolf Steiners Festschrift der „Erziehungskunst."* Verlag Freies Geistesleben, 1969.

Wiechert, Christof, "Rethinking the Threefold Division of

the Main Lesson." Translated by John Weedon. First published in the *Rundbrief* (Journal) of the Pedagogical Section, 2010. (Waldorf News: http://www.waldorftoday.com/2011/01/rethinking-the-threefold-division-of-the-main-lesson-christof-weichert/).

Acknowledgements

This book would not have been possible to write without the students I have had the privilege of teaching over the last three-plus decades. The experiences I gained through them have been invaluable to me on so many levels. The same holds true for the teachers who taught me, the mentors, colleagues, and the parents and guardians of the students. In this regard I am also greatly indebted to the Eugene Waldorf School and to Hawthorne Valley Waldorf School.

I especially want to acknowledge my late father, Willi Müller, who contributed substantially to Waldorf education in South Africa, Germany, and especially North America. He epitomized the essence of what it means to be a Waldorf teacher, and I am thankful for all the conversations we were able to have over the years regarding education and culture as such.

I would like to thank Patrick Stolfo and Leif Garbisch, for their close reading of the book, insightful suggestions, advice, editing recommendations, and encouraging words. I thank Marla Tolz for some of the photographs that appear in this book, including the cover. Thank you also to Helena Zay for the cover design and layout. I am grateful to the students who have granted me permission to use some of their artwork in this book, and hope that those I was not able to identify are happy to be included in this book. And, as always, I am greatly indebted to my wife, Martina Angela Müller for her incisive reading of the manuscript, the perceptive comments, and all the conversations we had on Waldorf education, particularly the role of the Main Lesson. Having attended a Waldorf School in Germany from kindergarten all the way through to the Abitur (13th year), she was able to critically assess the contents and offer important viewpoints for which I am truly grateful.

ILLUSTRATIONS

1) Taiko Drummer (Massimo Hamilton) p. xi
2) 8th Grade Science Project p. 17*
3) Bruce Frishkoff playing accordion p. 30*
4) 5th grade Classroom p. 35*
5) Children with leaf masks p. 42*
6) Francis of Assisi painting p. 50
7) Chinese Painting (Indigo Ocean) p. 55
8) Dancing Figures (Gabriel Lopez) p. 56
9) Egyptian Harpist p. 68
10) 7th Grade Circus p. 74*
11) Blackboard drawing of Aqueduct p. 81*
12) Dandelion p. 90
13) From a *Parzival* Main Lesson Book p. 95
14) Student and crayons p. 104*
15) Blackboard drawing of a Greek Myth p. 105*
16) Chinese Gong (Alexander Madey) p. 113
17) Dramatic reading of *Faust* (Magdalen Garrity, Berenika Lehrman) p. 129
18) Drawing of Gretchen (Gabriel Lopez) p. 136
19) Industrial Revolution (Indigo Ocean) p. 141
20) Blackboard drawing. 6th Grade Astronomy p. 160
21) Castle (Alexander Madey) p. 161
22) Scott Esty teaching Strings p. 170*
23) Still life p.195
24) Waldorf 100 (Photo: Michael Pewtherer) p. 197*
25) Egyptian Masks (5th grade) p. 200
26) Author Photo (Canaan Breiss)

* Photos by Marla Tolz

About the Author

Eric G. Müller is the director of Teacher Education at the Alkion Center, and a humanities teacher at the Hawthorne Valley Waldorf School in upstate New York. Born in Durban, South Africa, he studied literature and history at the University of the Witwatersrand, Johannesburg. He continued his studies at Emerson College, England, and the Institute for Waldorf Pedagogy in Witten-Annen, Germany, specializing in drama and music education. He took a class through the eight-year cycle in Eugene, Oregon, before becoming a Waldorf high school teacher. He has published numerous books, including novels, children's books, poetry, and a memoir.

ericgmuller.com

Made in the USA
Las Vegas, NV
21 March 2024

87561596R00118